LEADERSHIP REFLECTIONS

BY

PASTOR ANTHONY PAYTON

LP CHRISTIAN

ISBN 979-8-88831-689-4

TABLE OF CONTENTS

DEDICATION

So much of our lives are built on a continuum of people whose journeys have intersected ours during critical seasons. My opportunity to share my thoughts about leadership in these pages is no exception. I have been blessed beyond measure with relationships that have provided me with the social capital and life experiences to form the context in which these leadership reflections are presented.

At the forefront of these relationships is the one I share with my mother. She continued to believe in me, even when I gave her every reason to stop. I thank God for every remembrance of her and all she has been and is to me and others. Her example led me to a woman of like spirit to marry. Sandy has not only been my wife of 28 years and the mother of our children but a partner in the path that God has chosen for us. She has provided me a constant dose of vitamin E (encouragement) when I needed it most.

I have been blessed with two wonderful children. Zachary and Lydia are as much a part of the continuum as anyone—and they remain one of the most important reasons I have for getting this thing right in this life of mine. What I write here is for my children and my children's children's children. A life of servant leadership and a love for God and others is built into a child, not birthed into a child. This is why I believe the first test of my leadership is my children's lives.

This continuum would be incomplete without honoring five men that God strategically placed in my life when I needed leading from one point to another. E. C. (Buck) Mann led me to a relationship with the Lord while I was in a jail cell in Hattiesburg, Mississippi. He believed in me and convinced 19 others to believe in me and sign their names on a petition asking for my release. After the judge honored the petition, Buck mentored me for about three years and became the father I never had.

After Buck purchased a one-way ticket for me to come to Fort Wayne to go to school, I joined True Love Missionary Baptist Church under the leadership of Pastor Jesse White. Under his leadership, I became the Christian education director and learned many things about ministry in general, particularly in an inner-city context.

After enrolling in Fort Wayne Bible College, I answered an advertisement on the school board for a machine operating job. A gentleman by the name of Jack Fanning owned the company. Jack saw something in me and made me the plant manager of his company, mentoring me for five years. Jack showed me and taught me things about business that I could not have learned anywhere else.

After resigning from the Plant Manager position and struggling with finding a place to use my gift, God brought Pastor Ternae Jordan into my life. He provided me a stage to employ my gift, helping me realize I had value in the Kingdom.

After Pastor Jordan installed me as Pastor of Come As You Are Community Church and the church started to grow, God appointed Steve Stroup to my life. Steve not only sold me the house that had been his and Loretta's dream home, but for 11 years, he met with me each week for prayer. Even when his body was riddled with cancer, Steve would meet me and pray for me, my family, and the church.

I shudder to think where my life would be without all these people. I thank God I don't have to find out the answer to that question because they were there and continue to be there—if not physically, in spirit.

As my Brazilian friends would say, Deus é bom: *God is good*.

FOREWORD

I am honored and excited about writing the foreword to Leadership Reflections. I agree with John Maxwell, as stated in his book The 21 Irrefutable Laws of Leadership, "Everything rises and falls on leadership." Merriam-Webster defines leadership as "a position as a leader of a group, organization, etc.; the time when a person holds the position of leader; the power or ability to lead other people." Merriam-Webster also defines reflection as "an image that is seen in a mirror or a shiny surface; something that shows the effect, existence or character of something else."

In the spring of 1989, I was called to lead the Greater Progressive Baptist Church in Fort Wayne, Indiana. I was a young, frightened-but-enthusiastic pastor who had been called to enter new territory in a part of the country unfamiliar to me. Born a southern boy from the Volunteer State of Tennessee, I was raised in the home of a pastor who provided good godly leadership to many young preachers and pastors. He was a great example for me and others to observe and emulate.

In the early '90s, Fort Wayne was a community of churches in leadership transition. It was a city that was looking for progressive leadership to face various urban problems. In 1992, after being called to minister to two families who had lost children 15 years of age to street violence, I was introduced to a bright young minister by the name of Anthony Payton, who himself had been delivered from the claws of drugs and violence. He had become an excellent example for young men caught up in a negative lifestyle. He and I, and a young lady named Arlene Story, started a program called "Stop the Madness," which was designed to curb the acts of negative behavior by providing positive alternatives to life. "Stop the

Madness" became a national model for the US Justice Department Safe Cities Initiative.

Anthony and I ministered together and provided spiritual leadership to a community that was in a serious leadership shift. Together, hand in hand, we were able to transition a church and grow it from a membership of 25 to well over 2,500. On Sunday mornings, we would have 15-minutes of "Biblical Reflections." Payton would expound on biblical truths, and I would follow by preaching the Word of God. "Biblical Reflections" would provide biblical information to the congregation, and the preached Word would provide inspiration. Many lives were changed and won over for the Kingdom of God.

During that time, I watched this bright young man grow and develop into a strong leader both in the community and the church. As a result of his tremendous growth as a leader, in 1995, I had the pleasure of installing Anthony as the pastor of Come As You Are Community Church.

This book is a collection of challenging experiences that the author has overcome. These real-life reflections will provide a roadmap for future leaders, a set of challenges that have steered Anthony Payton to become the leader he is today. I have watched him mature and grow as a father, husband, mentor, pastor, and leader impacting many around the world.

While you benefit from Payton's hard-won wisdom, you will also learn that a good leader is derived from difficult times. Like Moses, he or she is aware that great leaders are developed through many traumatic experiences. As the author writes, "When you pray for rain, you must also be prepared to deal with the mud." Payton has dug his way out of the mud and "madness" and is now a dynamic leader who knows a reflective mirror designs his past to lead him into an abundant future. May you be blessed by his insights.

Dr. Ternae T. Jordan Sr. Senior Pastor, Mt. Canaan Baptist Church and Founder of "Stop the Madness" National

DAY 1

Lady in Red

I glanced over the shoulder of the young man that had stopped me to say hello and noticed Sandy seated at table number four. She must have felt me looking at her because, within seconds, she gracefully turned from the young lady she was talking to, and our eyes locked. Sandy smiled and gracefully returned to her conversation.

We have become accustomed to situations like this whenever we are out. We are well known in this place that I funnily refer to as Mayberry. So often, our eyes locked, and Sandy smiled as we continue our conversation with others individually. However, tonight her smile was different. Why? We were where she wanted to be, not where I had been invited to speak.

We've been married for 29 years, and I have been pastoring for 19 of those 29. Before that, I held leadership positions where I got called on and called away often. In the midst of all of that, both then and now, Sandy has kept her smile. However, tonight her smile was different; the evening was all about what she wanted to do and where she wanted to be.

Our children are grown and gone. Sandy and I in the house now—you know, the way husbands dream of it being. Where our children Zachary and Lydia once placed a smile on Sandy's face, today it is our granddaughters, Joanna and Jamila, who often make her smile. I am well acquainted with both of those smiles, but Sandy's smile was different tonight. She wasn't where she had to be for the kids, the grand girls, or me; she was where she wanted to be.

I stood there watching the young man's mouth move, but I couldn't tell you anything he said. I couldn't divorce myself from that smile. I remember collecting so many of my wife's smiles over the years. Many years ago, we were in a local hospital, and Sandy had just given birth to Zachary. After the Dr. placed Zachary in my arms and I cut the umbilical cord, the nurse took him from me and placed him in Sandy's arms. And there it was—that smile. The doctor invited me out so they could continue caring for Sandy and Zachary. "Give us about an hour," he said as I walked out. I realized I needed to get flowers for the occasion, so I took my delivery room gear off, washed up, and headed for the florists.

About an hour later, I returned with flowers in hand. The lights were low in the room, but I could see that Sandy had on this red nightgown, and like a scene from a movie, Chris de Burgh's song "The Lady in Red" was playing on the radio in the room. She heard me come in, looked at me, and there was that smile again. All I could see was Sandy in red with that smile as I listened to the song. It was an unforgettable moment.

Sandy wasn't wearing red tonight, but she was wearing that smile—and it beckoned for me. I gracefully ended my conversation with the young man, made my way to table number four, reached for Sandy's hand, and never left her side that night.

I have learned throughout the course of my life in leadership that the greatest legacy of my leadership is that smile on my wife's face. That's where the real value of my leadership is assessed. This should be the case for all that lead. We must major in family. Alex Haley is quoted as saying, "In every conceivable manner, the family is the link to our past and the bridge to our future." Leaders will do well to remember that. Ours is one of legacy building, not just career building, and it all starts with our family. I can't imagine being in leadership without Sandy, but more importantly, I can't imagine being married to anyone else but Sandy. She will always be my lady in red, no matter what color she's wearing.

So, when was the last time you put a smile on your spouse's face? Not the smile that is the result of them being where the children, grandchildren, or you need them to be, but a smile that's the result of them being where they want to be—which is with you. That smile that publicly approves of who you are because of who you are privately.

Leadership is not free! The price for it is your heart, and the first place you learn to pay that price is within your family. Yes, destiny may have decided that the two of you connect, but your heart decides if both of you will stay connected and in the other's heart.

Today, think about ways to show your family, especially your mate, your thanks for who they are and how they support what you have been called to do. Do at least one of these things today.

1. WHAT IS THE *PRINCIPLE* OF THE LESSON?

My takeaway from the lesson is...

____

____

____

____

____

____

2. WHAT IS THE *PRACTICE* FOR ME FROM THE LESSON?

I am committed to doing…

____

____

____

____

____

____

3. WHAT IS MY *PRAYER* AS A RESULT OF THE LESSON?

I am asking God to…

____

____

DAY 2

You Look Marvelous

I have never encountered a leader without scars. A leader's scars is the credit score of their leadership. The fewer scars a leader has, the lower the credit he or she is to their cause and call. Elbert Hubbard is quoted as saying, "God will not look you over for medals, degrees or diplomas, but for scars." I am convinced that you really don't know what leadership is until you have been patted on the shoulder and stabbed in the back by the same hand!

And that's real talk!

Much of today's leadership is more about comfort than scars. It's more about the prestige of leadership than the pain of leadership. It's more about the titles than the tears of leadership. Not only is this not a biblical paradigm, but it's not practical either.

In his book *Leadership and the Art of Struggle*, Steven Snyder writes:

Fulfilling your potential as a leader requires that you think differently about leadership. You must recast your struggles as positive learning experiences and view them as necessary steps in your development as a leader. You must look at leadership through an entirely different lens.

I have grown better from betrayal and not bitter. I have learned from the lies that have been told about me and to me. As a result, I have lingered less over the years at the "Slough of Despond." I like how Khalil Gibran states it: "Out of suffering have emerged the strongest souls; the most massive characters are seared with scars."

I often think about the fact that Jesus got up out of the grave, and yet he kept the nail prints! He kept his scars! For wherever the reality of this may take us theologically, there is at least one stop along the way that's practical: Thomas needed to see them!

John 20:25 (The Voice)

He heard the accounts of each brother's interaction with the Lord.

The Other Disciples: *We have seen the Lord!*

Thomas: *Until I see His hands, feel the wounds of the nails, and put my hand to His side, I won't believe what you are saying.*

A leader's scars are for public consumption. We wear and own them for ourselves and others: not out of some sense of false piety or ego-inflated pride; not to become demigods; but to demonstrate the power of our God. As a result, no one will have to look back and wonder how we got over; they will know that God brought us over and out!

In the recurring "Fernando's Hideaway" sketch of Saturday Night Live, Billy Crystal used Fernando Lamas' accent for inspiration, and a quote from the actor: "It is better to look good than to feel good." You may not feel good about your scars, but you can look good wearing them.

So, wear your scars as well as you wear Prada, Armani, or Dolce and Gabbana, because your scars were designed for you. And you look marvelous!

1. WHAT IS THE *PRINCIPLE* OF THE LESSON?

My takeaway from the lesson is...

____

____

____

____

____

____

2. WHAT IS THE _PRACTICE_ FOR ME FROM THE LESSON?

I am committed to doing…

____

____

____

____

____

____

3. WHAT IS MY _PRAYER_ AS A RESULT OF THE LESSON?

I am asking God to…

____

____

____

____

____

____

DAY 3

There are No Sidelines, Just Sides

I sat nervously, staring at the beauty of the office. I had never seen anything like it. Even though the office building as a whole was not in use anymore, it was apparent that we were sitting in what was once the CEO's office. Dark walnut wood was everywhere, and there was even a fireplace. My wonder was interrupted by the voice of my pastor, Dr. Jesse White: "Payton, we need you to take notes."

There I sat, among four of the most regarded leaders of our community: Dr. Vernon Graham, Dr. Mike Necklson, Dr. Bleedso, and Dr. Jesse White. Two other men sat there, too, though I had never heard of them before. However, I knew immediately they were businessmen of the community, and I could tell they were from "old money." After that day, I never forgot their names.

The scene was fitting—older men, in an old room with old money. I felt like a kid in a Western, standing on the side, watching famous gunslingers face off at high noon. The contrast to this was me, a young man with no money.

I gathered my notepad when one of the men said, "We prefer no notes, please." I looked at Dr. White, and he said, "Payton, it's OK, put it away." As soon as I did, one of the businessmen said, "Look, gentlemen, we really would like this project to go forth, and we need your help." "We understand," responded pastor Graham, "but the community doesn't want it."

"We believe the community is misinformed," responded one of the businessmen. The conversation went back and forth for what seemed like hours. So much so, I said to myself, '*What am I doing here? I could be back at the office working*'... Amid my internal dialogue, one of the businessmen said the magic words: "We are prepared to do whatever it takes."

"We have talked," continued the businessman, "and we would like to set up a fund that will pay you guys $60,000 per month for ten years, and we are prepared to give the first $60,000 today." You do the math. I was blown away, as this sum seemed even larger when this happened nearly thirty years ago. At 26, I realized the gravity of the situation.

Quickly surveying the faces of the men, I was with, Dr. Graham turned red and, in unison with the other community leaders, said, "We don't want your money!" Dr. White continued, "We live in this community, and we serve the people of this community—and if they don't want it, we are not going to force it upon them. This meeting is over, gentlemen."

We shook hands with the businessman and walked out. Riding home in a car with Dr. White, I sat silently. When we pulled out of the gate of the complex, he asked me, "Payton, what did you learn?" I didn't answer his question. Instead, I responded, "Pastor, you don't think there is a way to make this happen, that's a lot of money to leave on the table . . . maybe if we sideline this and come back to it later, the community will feel different about it." Then came the leadership lesson of a lifetime. Pastor White said, "I asked you what you learned, not what we can do." "Payton," he continued, "There are some things where there is no sideline—just sides—and this is one of them."

I never forgot that meeting. More importantly, I never forgot that lesson. In my own leadership sphere, I've never encountered a more expensive example of leading well. Leadership is about standing up for what is right, no matter the cost. Standing on the sidelines is never an option for a leader.

When we make decisions based on making a living, we will never make a life. While we may comfort ourselves that we "bring home a good check," we continue to die on the inside. Regarding issues of truth and principles, I've learned that "compromise" is a four-letter word. Thomas Jefferson is quoted as saying, "In matters of style, swim with the current; in matters of principle, stand like a rock."

1. WHAT IS THE *PRINCIPLE* OF THE LESSON?

My takeaway from the lesson is...

____

____

____

____

____

____

2. WHAT IS THE *PRACTICE* FOR ME FROM THE LESSON?

I am committed to doing…

____

____

____

____

____

____

3. WHAT IS MY _PRAYER_ AS A RESULT OF THE LESSON?

I am asking God to…

____

____

____

____

____

____

DAY 4

A Valuable Lesson

One of the most valuable lessons I have ever learned as a leader came while I was lying flat on my back on the canvas of life.

I was there as a result of being sucker-punched with such repetitive force that even my pride shouted from my corner, "Stay down, stay down, stay down!" I recall not only wanting to throw in the towel but reaching for the entire laundry basket full of towels to throw in! The most devastating aspect of my time on the canvas was the fact that friends had placed me there. Friends threw the punches. Yes, friends! It wasn't accidental friendly fire; this was a deliberate assault from those close to me. In the words of King David, "Even my friend, in whom I trusted, one who ate my bread, has raised his heel against me." (Psalm 41 HCSB)

Under what seemed like a collaborative effort to destroy me, my family, the church I served, and everything we had built and was working on; I felt like I was collapsing. One by one, many of my so-called friends played "Rock 'Em Sock 'Em Robots" with my dreams.

These were people I had brought into my inner circle. I paid their rent, water bills, electric bills, gas bills, and even paid for family vacations. I loaned money, gave cars, and gave money to them to purchase cars. They were my team and repaid me by teaming up against me. They stole from me and lied about me. When asked why, they replied, "*I was mad.*" I am convinced that things would have been worse if it had not been for the grace of God and the little thing called the record button. Now that's another story for another day.

The scars of that experience have faded, and the lessons I learned are legion. The most valuable lesson came as I sat and lamented the situation with one of my mentors. I asked him why he thought they had done this to me. His answer was both healing and hurtful. He said, "Payton when people only see what's in your hand, they will neither validate nor value what's in your heart."

Did you get that? Let me repeat it: "When people only see what's in your hand, they will neither validate nor value what's in your heart." It was an eye-opening ray of light, and with it, I found what I had been looking for. I wept until I had no strength to weep anymore.

Those of us who lead with our heart (and I can't imagine a leader leading another way) don't just loan money, pay someone's bills, or send families on vacations. Those things are the condiments that go along with a serving heart. They are the mint jelly that goes along with the lamb. They are our heart's way of giving our hand a purpose. And therein is the reason for the pain: in the validation of our heart. For the most part, we care less about the things taken from our hands. To invalidate a leader's heart is to render them invisible in your sight. Believe me, every leader wants to be seen for their heart, not the fishes and loaves in their hand.

It is also true that every leader will feel the sting of betrayal—and unfortunately, it will come more often than not from friends. You know that, don't you? You have felt that sting, haven't you? You are feeling those stings even now, aren't you? I can hear you shouting, "Yes, yes, yes! But what do I do about it?"

As much as the sting of betrayal is a part of the leadership experience, and as much as others may settle for what's in a leader's hand rather than validating and valuing a leader's heart, leaders must guard their hearts against bitterness and all related diseases. They do this by forgiving the violators. Trust me! A leader may muscle his or her way through, but they won't move on until they have forgiven.

Please remember that Jesus' forgiveness preceded the resurrection. I know that this is hard! I have been there! "Men are more ready to repay an injury," says Tacitus, "than a benefit because gratitude is a burden and revenge a pleasure."

For me, my desire to please God demanded that I forgive. And I wanted to live so that when my children and my children's children thought of fairness and integrity, they would think of me. I also owed the people who stuck with me a better leader, not a bitter leader.

1. WHAT IS THE _PRINCIPLE_ OF THE LESSON?

My takeaway from the lesson is...

____

____

____

____

____

____

2. WHAT IS THE PRACTICE FOR ME FROM THE LESSON?

I am committed to doing…

____

____

____

____

____

____

3. WHAT IS MY _PRAYER_ AS A RESULT OF THE LESSON?

I am asking God to…

____

____

____

DAY 5

Distant Lover

I am a child of the '70s, and I still enjoy listening to much of the music from those days. Many of the songs from the '70s serve as an umbilical cord to my childhood dreams—a time when childlike faith overruled the objections of others to keep those dreams alive. There is something about the spirit of music that does that. Songs can stimulate our romantic impulses, turn our darkness into day and simultaneously march us into battle—all in one two-minute, 45-second song.

One day, after spending time at Starbucks reading and writing, I decided along the way home to stop and wash my car. After pulling out of the wash, I pulled over to a space allotted for those who wanted to dry their cars by hand. I dried my car off, cleaned the mats, and conditioned the leather—there is nothing like a clean black car. I was feeling good. In the words of the rapper Ice Cube, "It was a good day."

After cleaning, drying, and conditioning my car, I let the sunroof back, lowered the two front windows, adjusted my radio to SiriusXM "The Groove," and pulled off. In a manner of seconds, Marvin Gaye's song 'Distant Lover' came on, and I thought, *It can't get any better.* I smiled and bopped my head up and down. (And by the way, I still love Jesus!) I mean, a clean black man, in a clean black car, on a clear and sunny day, listening to the smooth sounds of Marvin Gaye . . . How would you feel?

As I cruised down the Jefferson as though I were the only one on the road, I started listening to the lyrics more and the music less. I tried to sing along—no one else was in the car, so I could get away with that. There was one line I couldn't get out of my head when Marvin sang about his woman being many miles away and his longing for her. The line I couldn't get out of my head was:

Distant lover, lover

So many miles away,

Heaven knows that I long for you,

Every night, every night,
and sometimes I yearn
Through the day

I believe 1974 is the year that song was released. Distant Lover was the sixth song on the "Let's Get It On" album and the "B" side of the second single from the album "Come Get To This." The live version—which was now playing on my radio, was recorded in 1974 and is probably the best live recorded song in music history.

I know Marvin was singing about a woman, but I was a 14-year-old dreamer, living in Mississippi at the time and listening to the song. To this day, the tune takes me back to my dreams of 42 years ago. As I thought about those dreams and those days, I was soon caught up in euphoria.

However, it wasn't long before remembering the reality of so many of those dreams not coming true caused me to view *Distant Lover* not as Marvin's song about a woman but a song about my dreams.

If you have been a leader for a while—and lived beyond fourteen, you know what it's like to view some dreams as distant lovers. Perhaps, some of your dreams are so distant that you have even stopped investing in them and given your affections to another. Am I right about it?

What is another, you ask? A job that you really don't like. A clock you are using to punch in rather than a clock you own, a place you are renting rather than one you own, a ministry you are in rather than a mission you are on.

Should I go on? Maybe you've settled for a church that you are pastoring rather than a church that you are leading, a marriage you are tolerating rather than a marriage you are thrilled to be in, a life of depression rather than a life of destiny, a relationship you have accepted rather than believing yourself as worthy of another! I think you get the picture. Am I right?

There is a period of time about which, Sydney Harris says, "Enemies, as well as lovers, come to resemble each other over a period of time." For leaders, that's the period where our dreams become distant lovers and the memories—in the words of Barbra Streisand—remind us of "the way we were."

Lord, may our dreams not become distant lovers and where they have, please teach us to reverence them again.

1. WHAT IS THE _PRINCIPLE_ OF THE LESSON?

My takeaway from the lesson is...

____

____

____

____

____

2. WHAT IS THE _PRACTICE_ FOR ME FROM THE LESSON?

I am committed to doing…

____

____

____

____

____

3. WHAT IS MY _PRAYER_ AS A RESULT OF THE LESSON?

I am asking God to…

____

____

____

____

____

____

DAY 6

Feeding Frenzy

I love the study of words. As far back as I can remember, I have always asked those who were speaking, especially my mother, "What does this word mean?" when I didn't know. Now that I communicate for a living, I have finally realized why that hunger was there.

Once, in preparation for a talk, I was looking for a way to communicate an idea vividly, so I thought about the phrase "feeding frenzy." I had heard the phrase before but didn't know the etymology of it. My mother wasn't around, so I consulted Wikipedia. I learned that in ecology, a feeding frenzy is a situation where oversaturation of a supply of food leads to rapid feeding by predatory animals. For example, a large school of fish can cause nearby sharks to enter a feeding frenzy. This can cause the sharks to go wild, biting anything that moves, including each other.

Well, the phrase feeding frenzy turned out to be overkill for the context of my talk. However, I couldn't get that picture out of my mind; as situational providence would have it, a context emerged where it was most fitting.

Months later, I received a call from a friend. Our mutual network of friends, Facebook, and Twitter feeds had been ablaze with news concerning his fall. To be completely honest, I knew what it was about when I saw his name and number on my caller ID. As the phone continued to ring, I stared at his name and number and debated whether or not I should answer it. Then suddenly, the thought occurred to me that I hadn't prayed for him and his family since I had heard about the situation, so the least I could do was answer his call! I did.

A 'hello' from me was all it took, and the floodgates were opened; he cried and cried and cried! Over the next few months, we talked often. Then he said one day: "This situation has become a feeding frenzy, and the only safe place I have is with you." At that moment, I was completely ashamed for the seconds I debated and delayed answering his call. For those few seconds, I willingly participated in the feeding frenzy. Adding to my shame was the fact that none of the allegations were true. The person that started it all later admitted that she had lied because she was angry about being fired! But of course, by now, the damage was already done.

By design, the sound byte in the society in which we now live, divorces us from context. It's all about the headline and not the heart. We'd rather gurgle from the bottle of sensationalism than sip from the cup of substance because taking the time to fact-check delays the news and allows for the possibility of someone else beating us to the story or at least to the posting.

Gutter journalism, both electronic and printed, has become the norm, and virtually no story is absent of malice. Gossip dresses itself up in a flashy blog and calls itself news, and before you can say, "check, please," someone has linked it to their Twitter or Facebook feed and has legitimatized a lie. Thus, a feeding frenzy.

As leaders, we must guard ourselves against participation in feeding frenzies against others in general and leaders in particular. We must stop being predatory animals and start being purveyors of truth in love. This process begins with our own feeding habits. I believe there are entirely too many good books for leaders to feed from rather than a troth of gossip! If you feed on gossip, you will become a gossiper. If you spend more time on blogs than in the Bible, you will have a bloggers' perspective rather than God's perspective.

A Native American grandfather was talking to his grandson about how he felt. He said, "I feel as if I have two wolves fighting in my heart. One wolf is the vengeful, angry, and violent one, while the other wolf is the loving and compassionate one." The grandson asked, "Which wolf will win the fight in your heart?" The grandfather answered, "The one I feed."

Which one will you feed today?

1. WHAT IS THE *PRINCIPLE* OF THE LESSON?

My takeaway from the lesson is...

____

____

____

____

____

2. WHAT IS THE *PRACTICE* FOR ME FROM THE LESSON?

I am committed to doing...

____

____

____

____

____

3. WHAT IS MY *PRAYER* AS A RESULT OF THE LESSON?

I am asking God to...

____

____

____

____

____

DAY 7

Respect the Process

I stood in the lobby of the Bahia Principe Privilege Club in Punta Cana, Dominican Republic. I was there for some much-needed rest. This was my first time in Punta Cana, and so far, I was very impressed with the accommodations. The staff was outstanding, and they truly made me feel privileged to be there.

Everything was going well until they asked me to pay twenty-eight percent more in taxes. This request came at the same time the gentleman informed me that my room wasn't available yet. All of a sudden, I no longer felt privileged. The fact that the room was not ready, wasn't a deal breaker, but the request that I pay twenty-eight percent in taxes was! I protested paying these taxes. At this point, I felt more Republican than I had felt in almost eight years!

"I paid for this entire vacation before I departed the States," I said. "Here is my receipt." "Yes, Mr. Payton, but they didn't charge you the taxes, and now that you are here, the taxes have doubled." He continued, "If you had paid, while you were still in the States, the taxes would only be fourteen percent." "OK, I will get on the Internet and pay the fourteen percent." "Mr. Payton, you can't do that because we know that you are already here." Upon hearing this, I responded in a classic American tone, "I need to speak to a manager, PLEASE!" "OK, Mr. Payton," the young man said.

Not long after he had gone behind a set of closed doors, he emerged with an attractive lady, who stretched out her hand and said, "Hello, Mr. Payton, my name is Carline, and I am the manager." "Nice to meet you, Carline," I said publicly while saying to myself privately, '*I don't care how good you look; I am not paying twenty-eight percent in taxes.*'

I explained the situation; she went to the computer, pulled up my reservation, and said, "Yes, Mr. Payton, for some reason, they didn't collect the taxes on this reservation, and now that you are here, the government demands that we take the amount of taxes that the locals would have to pay."

"What!" I protested. "Refund my money, and I will fly back to the States!" (Yes, I know that was crazy since I did say I was in need of some much-needed rest.) Carline remained calm and said, "Mr. Payton, this isn't worth you canceling your vacation." I sounded back with, "It's an issue of principle!" And without raising her voice, she checked and mated me. "I understand it is a matter of principle, Mr. Payton, but please respect the process." I smiled and said, "You are good." We both laughed, I paid the taxes, and they treated me like a king!

"Respect the Process." How many times had I taught others to do that? Now the teacher had to be reminded of his own lesson plan. Leaders must learn to respect the process in their personal and professional lives. The law of process is vital to what we do and who we become. Yet, while most of us are ready to cry aloud about respecting the principle, we disrespect the law of process. We often lose sight of the fact that how we climb the mountain is just as important as climbing the mountain. It is worth noting that God, who could have spoken and created the world in one day, chose to spread the work over a process of six days, and not one thing was done before its time during the process.

As a leader, the most important thing you may do today is join yourself to the process. The process is important regardless of the outcome. We cannot sacrifice the process on the altar of the destination. It is as much about the drive there as it is arriving there, and our life principles become our tour guides. And yes, I am aware that the process can get boring; still, we must value building a foundation over frantic movement.

I am thankful that Carline reminded me to respect the process. I am in her debt, a debt that I can only pay through the discipline that comes with respecting the process. Thanks to her, it is a debt that I fully intend to pay while paying it forward.

1. WHAT IS THE _PRINCIPLE_ OF THE LESSON?

My takeaway from the lesson is...

____

____

____

____

____

2. WHAT IS THE _PRACTICE_ FOR ME FROM THE LESSON?

I am committed to doing…

____

____

____

____

____

3. WHAT IS MY _PRAYER_ AS A RESULT OF THE LESSON?

I am asking God to…

____

____

____

____

DAY 8

Adding Value

It was Monday, August 4, 2014, at 6:59 pm. The ding from my iPad went off and alerted me that I had a message from a Facebook friend.

Usually, I take my time looking into these messages, but it was Monday, my day off, and I had been lying around the house all day. So, I took the time and energy to investigate. To my surprise, it was a message from Derrick, one of my cousins from Mississippi. Given that we don't talk that much and that his mother, the "Buttermilk Pie" queen of the family, had been sick for a long time, just seeing his name put me in a state of emergency.

After reading the first sentence, I was relieved that it wasn't bad news about my aunt. Instead, it was a personal request for direction for his life. I asked him for permission to share a portion of his message here, and he consented. So here it is, in his own words:

How are you doing? I know we don't talk very much, but you are the only man, other than granddaddy, that I have ever looked up to. You know I'm really not the one to talk about my personal life . . . but I need someone I respect to give me some guidance. I come to you lost, and I have no idea what to do.

Anyone with any idea of what his words meant to me, they would have to know that Derrick was the first person I tried to lead to a relationship with Christ over 30 years ago. I was just coming out of the dark night of my soul myself and wanted to share the light with someone. Derrick was the youngest of us four cousins of our grandmother's three daughters.

The other cousins—Greg, Dell, and I—had experienced the benefit of time to do something with our lives. Though truthfully, neither Greg nor Dell had done as much as I had to destroy their lives. That being said, it felt like a mandate upon my life to make it very difficult for Derrick to do what I had done or take after me. I took him to church, shared Christ with him, and then I moved to Fort Wayne.

Later, as a young adult man, he phoned and asked for my help, and I did what I could.

Our journey together started when Derrick was four, and I was about 24. Now that he was 34 and I was 56, after years of not talking, he reached out at the very season when I was reflecting upon whether I had made a difference in anyone's life.

As leaders, we live in a world of results—and immediate results at that. Ours are timeframes and deadlines, spreadsheets, and profit margins. However, as Derrick's message reminded me, the true impact of our leadership can't be fully measured by timeframes and deadlines, spreadsheets, and profit margins. It's not about the ledger but more about God leveraging our life in a way that brings profit to time and eternity. Paul wrote, "One-man plants, one-man waters, but God brings increase."

Our chief goal as leaders is to add value by planting, watering, and trusting God for increase. We can't do this without a proper understanding of human dignity. R. C. Sproul assesses human dignity in these terms:

Man's dignity rests in God, who assigns an inestimable worth to every person. Man's origin is not an accident but a profoundly intelligent act by one who has eternal value, by one who stamps His own image on each person. God creates men and moves heaven and earth to redeem them when they fall. Our origin is in the creation, and our destiny is for redemption. Between these points, every human heartbeat has value.

Leaders add value, and as you know, there are millions in need of it. This was the cry from Derrick as he continued in his message to me:

I'm not making enough money to do the things for my family that I need to do. I've tried to find a second job but no one will hire me. My marriage is at a bad place right now because we have no idea how to be married or any idea how to fix it. I still pray and talk to God on a regular basis like you taught me to, but I can't attend church because on Sunday mornings I'm working.

I'm just at a place in my life where I feel lost and alone, even in my own home. I feel like everyone is against me, and they're looking and waiting for me to fail in life. As a man, I just really need the experience of someone I respect to help me and guide me so that I can be the man that I know God has put me here to be. So, I come to you for help.

The Bible says, "God so loved the world that he gave his only begotten Son" (John 3:16 KJV). Ladies and gentlemen, that's a value-adding statement. God is a value-adding leader in creation and in man's fall. And I believe what He did for the world, He would have done for one. In other words, if the world's population had been made up of only you, God would have done the same.

What about you? Today, will you go out of your way for one? Will you be a value-adding leader? Someone like Derrick is looking and hoping for your guidance and encouragement, and that person probably isn't far away. Will you go out of your way for the one?

1. WHAT IS THE *PRINCIPLE* OF THE LESSON?

My takeaway from the lesson is...

____

____

____

____

____

____

2. WHAT IS THE _PRACTICE_ FOR ME FROM THE LESSON?

I am committed to doing…

____

____

____

____

____

____

3. WHAT IS MY _PRAYER_ AS A RESULT OF THE LESSON?

I am asking God to…

____

____

____

____

____

____

DAY 9

Hunt

I grew up in Hattiesburg, Mississippi. There, I experienced some of life's good, bad, and ugly. I have some of the most memorable times from that period, despite the rough times involved in hunting and fishing.

In fact, waking up at 1:00 am to travel to the Gulf Port to fish still puts a smile on my face. Being a son of the South automatically qualified you for a shotgun; on my tenth birthday, my grandmother bought me one. Yes, I did say my grandmother. Rabbit hunting was the bomb, and I was even good at it.

Not long after receiving this 410-gauge shotgun, a more experienced hunter, Mr. Dean, gave me a Blue-Tick hound dog. Blue—that's the name I gave her—was my first hunting dog. Though I had a German Shepherd and a Collie before, I now owned a full-blooded Blue Tick hunting dog! Imagine my delight.

At the time, where we lived was considered the country, so I didn't technically have to wake up at 1:00 am to go hunting. I just walked out of our back door. So, I conveniently decided to take my Blue-Tick hound dog for a hunting spin. I walked out the back door with my new 410-gauge shotgun, untied Blue, and started for the field.

However, there was something a little puzzling about Blue's reaction to the field. She just hung around my leg. There was no excitement about being in the field. I would say, "Gittum girl!" but there was no wagging of her tail and no "gittum." She wouldn't hunt!

After pressing Blue to hunt for what seemed like hours, I finally gave up and returned home. Disappointed and disgusted, I waited to see the gentleman that gave her to me to give him a piece of my mind. (At least as much of a piece of my mind a ten-year-old was allowed to give an adult in an African American family living in the South in 1968, which was very, very little.) Oh my, how much times have changed.

I saw Mr. Dean later that day and proceeded to share with him; you honestly didn't tell adults anything in the South, especially the era and area I grew up in. He said, "Oh, I thought I told you she was gun-shy; she's afraid of hunting." I responded, "I already have a pet; I thought you were giving me a hunting dog."

Ed Dean gave me that adult look, and my grandmother, who had heard me, came out of the house. When I heard the screen door slam behind her, I knew I had gone too far with my comments. "I'm sorry, Mr. Dean, I did not mean any disrespect. Thank you for the dog."

I was fortunate; this time, I got by with a tongue lashing instead of a physical lashing from my grandmother. And I accepted my fate. I kept Blue for a pet, and she never hunted.

I believe it is safe to say, leaders sometimes become gun-shy. Gun-shy is an adjective that describes a human or animal who is hesitant, wary, or distrustful, especially because of previous unpleasant experiences. Our previous bad experiences can cause us to shrink away from what we have been designed to become. Our inherent nature for the hunt is replaced with the comfort of what has been hunted. In the past, others would have told us "Slow down" because of our excitement, but instead, people are now asking, "What happened to you?"

Nothing is as sad as a leader who mistakes passivity with strategic thinking. These leaders were once powerful teachers of leadership in learning and lifestyle. However, now they are satisfied with being the teacher's pet in their own classroom. They are gun-shy! They are unfortunately hesitant, wary, or distrustful, especially because of previous unpleasant experiences.

If this is you today, please hear my passionate cry from these pages, "We need you! We can't hunt without you!" Arise, mighty man or woman of God, and get your hunt on! You can become a leadership enthusiast again. Hang a sign on the door of your previous bad experiences and your current hesitations, wariness, and distrust that reads, "Gone Huntin'!"

So you have missed some shots in the past. God doesn't care that you are not a big shot or the best shot. Hang your hunting sign anyway, and remember the words of Teddy Roosevelt: "No, I'm not a good shot, but I shoot often." Now hunt!

1. WHAT IS THE *PRINCIPLE* FOR ME FROM THE LESSON?

My takeaway from the lesson is...

____

____

____

____

____

____

2. WHAT IS THE *PRACTICE* FOR ME FROM THE LESSON?

I am committed to doing…

____

____

____

____

____

3. WHAT IS MY *PRAYER* AS A RESULT OF THE LESSON?

I am asking God to…

____

____

____

DAY 10

If You Think You're Lonely Now…

How deep is your well?

Every leader will face challenges where they will instantly attempt to draw from the wells of their experiences to resolve a matter in front of them. They might even push us to leap tall obstacles with a single bound. However, at other times these experiences seem to weaken us like Kryptonite. Thankfully, on the leadership journey, there are times when these challenges become our Superheroes, dramatically coming to our rescue.

There have been times in leadership in general and pastoring in particular where having grown up as an only child has helped me tremendously. For instance, I grew up as an only child; therefore, I learned to play marbles by myself, and I learned to be my "chief company keeper" as we would say in the South. When I needed the type of clarity that only comes in isolation, it was easy for me to transition to that state of being. When I needed to regain focus, and I knew how others would view my ability to disconnect and become anti-social, my experiences as an only child empowered me to disconnect regardless so easily. When I needed to do what God was calling me to do, which was not what others wanted me to do, my experiences as an only child allowed me to pick up my marbles and go home without any animosity.

However, there has been one area in my leadership experience that has been Kryptonite to my "only child" experiences. Loneliness! One would think that growing up as an only child would have built up my immunity against loneliness, but this is not so. Leadership is, in fact, a magnet to loneliness, and loneliness is its Kryptonite! In a November 4, 1969, speech entitled "The Loneliness of Leadership," Gordon B. Hinckley made the following observations:

The price of leadership is loneliness. The price of adherence to conscience is loneliness. The price of adherence to principle is loneliness. I think it is inescapable. The Savior of the world was a man who walked in loneliness. I do not know of any statement more underlined with the pathos of loneliness than His statement: "The foxes have holes, and the birds of the air have nests; but the Son of man hath not where to lay his head (Matthew 8:20 KJV).

With every leadership step we take comes an inevitable increase in loneliness. The higher we climb in leadership, the more responsibilities we have, and in many instances, the lonelier we become. No matter how publicly popular a leader may be, he or she suffers from loneliness more than most people would dare to believe. If you are going to lead, you will have seasons of loneliness and, sometimes, prolonged seasons of loneliness. The reality is if you think you are lonely now, wait until you start leading!

Consider William Shakespeare's words in King Henry IV, Part II: "Uneasy lays the head that wears a crown." We see the reality of this in the earthly life of King Jesus. Two of the most intense times in Jesus' earthly ministry are marked by loneliness: in the garden, before his trial where He couldn't pull together a three-hour prayer meeting, and on the cross as he cries out, saying, *"Eli, Eli, lama sabachthani?"* That is, "My God, My God, why hast Thou forsaken Me?"

As I have contemplated these two intense seasons of loneliness in my Lord's life, I have considered the intense seasons of loneliness in my own leadership and those mentioned in conversations with other leaders. My conclusion is this: there seem to be two seasons in which leaders experience intense loneliness. First is the transition to a new direction in your life; the second is a time of tremendous sacrifice to secure that new direction in your life. Those are the times when the tables tend to turn in a dramatic way. So, if you think you are lonely now, in the words of the late Bobby Womack, "Wait until tonight."

So, what is a leader to do in these intense seasons of loneliness? Be prepared to keep hope in you and before you! When cheers have turned into boos, allow the hope within you to give you a standing ovation! When friends walk out, leave the door open so new ones can walk in! When depression beckons, allow a determination to drive it away.

When those that once wanted to crown you now want to crucify you, take a lesson from our Lord, and don't let that stop you! Persevere with the help of the Creator of the universe—the one who knows each star and counts each grain of sand on the seashore—and your future will become brighter after times of loneliness.

1. WHAT IS THE _PRINCIPLE_ OF THE LESSON?

My takeaway from the lesson is...

---

2. WHAT IS THE PRACTICE FOR ME FROM THE LESSON?

I am committed to doing…

____

____

____

____

____

3. WHAT IS MY PRAYER AS A RESULT OF THE LESSON?

I am asking God to…

____

____

____

____

____

DAY 11

No Excuses

A huge rivalry exists in Louisiana college basketball between the University of Louisville and the University of Kentucky. The following story clearly illustrates the intensity of the competition. During one of those "Dream Games" between the two schools, an elderly woman was sitting alone with an empty seat next to her. A young man approached and said, "Ma'am, I have rarely seen an empty seat in Rupp Arena, let alone at the Dream Game. Whose seat is this?"

The woman responded by explaining that she and her husband had been season ticket holders for 28 years and that the seat had belonged to him. "Well," said the young man, couldn't you have found a friend or relative to come to the game with you?" "Are you kidding?" she replied. "They're all at my husband's funeral."

It's a joke that's easy to laugh at, and though this basketball fan's priority could be questioned, the one thing that can't be questioned is her commitment.

No matter how gifted a leader may be, their gifts cannot come before their commitment! Commitment is a five-cent word with a million-dollar price tag. A leader's disposition about the price provides a room with a view for all to see what it means to put your hands to the plow and not look back.

As leaders in general and gifted leaders in particular, there are those seasons when we feel like Reggie Jackson in a perpetual October. The curveball we didn't expect comes in low; before we know it, it's strike one and then strike two. In these times, the only thing that keeps us swinging is commitment! And suddenly, we receive the revelation and the realization that we are either just interested fans or committed participants in the plan of God.

Art Turock, in his book *Getting Physical,* writes, "There's a difference between interest and commitment. When you are interested in doing something, you do it only when circumstances permit. When you are committed to doing something, you accept no excuses, only result."

There it is—no excuses—the heartbeat of this five-cent word with the million-dollar price tag. Sadly, much of today's leadership vacuum is filled with superstar leaders who are more interested in the crown of the position rather than the commitment to the practice. Too many of us are only interested in the things of God as long as the road is easy.

Please pause for a moment and allow me perhaps to be the first to tell you; that there will be times in your leadership experience where there is no road, and the only path you have is the one you leave behind you!

Now that's real talk!

As leaders, we must be perpetually reminded that the only thing that costs us more than the five-cent word with a million-dollar price tag is *excuses*. When Dr. David Livingston was working in Africa, a group of his friends wrote him, stating, "We would like to send other men to you. Have you found a good road into your area yet?" According to a family member, Dr. Livingston sent this message in reply, "If you have men who will only come if they know there is a good road, I don't want them. I want men who will come if there is no road at all."

So here is a declaration, a battle cry if you will . . .

As a leader, I will neither entertain any new nor sustain any old excuses. Whatever the situation, from this day forward and by the power of God, it's deuces to all excuses!

1. WHAT IS THE *PRINCIPLE* OF THE LESSON?
My takeaway from the lesson is...

____

____

____

____

____

____

2. WHAT IS THE _PRACTICE_ FOR ME FROM THE LESSON?
I am committed to doing…

____

____

____

____

3. WHAT IS MY _PRAYER_ AS A RESULT OF THE LESSON?
I am asking God to…

____

____

____

____

DAY 12

Tell Me Something Good

A few months ago, I was flooded by a wave of bad news. In many ways, it seems like it was just yesterday, and it certainly couldn't have come at a more inopportune time. Of course, bad news never comes at an opportune time.

I have received bad news before, but this time it not only circled the globe of my world, it landed on the runway of my heart—and it was a hard landing. Like skilled pilots, those that brought me this bad news tried to keep the nose of it up, but the force of it was too much. Like a tale from the life of Job, while the words were still in the mouth of one, another showed up with more bad news.

At this point, I was emotionally, intellectually, physically, and spiritually drained. Over the course of the days that followed, I questioned my very call—especially within the context of the place I was called to serve. Doubt, disgust, and dare I say it, depression settled in for the kill. Here I was the leader who had spoken prophetically to many with no prophetic words for himself.

The Word of God declares, "A prophet has no honor in his own home." As mind-blowing as that may be, I think there are seasons when a prophet and, or leader has no honor in his own heart! There are those seasons where any given leader doubts themselves, their call, and most importantly, the God that has called them for such a time as this!

The intensity and reality of bad news and leadership struggles, in general, can do that to all of us. Leaders are curators and prognosticators of the prophetic. That is, they deal with the forth telling and foretelling of the world they have been called to impact. However, when the honor of this call and office is lost within their own heart, if they find they can't speak life to themselves, we all lose!

There isn't a leader that has ever led anything that has not had to deal with bad news and the threat against their prophetic voice. The French General, politician, and emperor Napoleon Bonaparte had a unique perspective on bad news. He said, "Never awake me when you have good news to announce because with good news nothing presses; but when you have bad news, arouse me immediately, for then there is not an instant to be lost." Therein lies the reality of a leader's response to bad news: "arouse immediately."

The very thought and disposition I have no time to waste speak to the prophetic voice that should reside in every leader no matter how bad the news may be. The first step is to arouse immediately and simultaneously encourage yourself in the LORD. I am encouraging you to speak prophetically to yourself.

"But what am I to say?" you ask. How about starting with this: "Self, tell me something good. Remind me again of who I am in Christ and that greater is He that is in me than he that is in the world. Remind me that I am more than a conqueror and that my God shall supply my every need!"

Jay Leno, of The Tonight Show fame, tells the following joke in one of his monologues. "An Israeli man's life was saved when he was given a Palestinian man's heart in a heart transplant operation. The guy is doing fine, but the bad news is, he can't stop throwing rocks at himself."

As leaders, we must walk away from the rock pile and stop throwing rocks at ourselves when bad things or bad news come our way. Even when we are not the prophet in our own home, we must be the prophet with honor in our own hearts. In the words of Joseph Campbell, "Find a place inside where there's joy, and the joy will burn out the pain."

Arouse immediately, man or woman of God. Tell yourself something good in these moments because your destiny awaits you and depends upon it!

1. WHAT IS THE _PRINCIPLE_ OF THE LESSON?

My takeaway from the lesson is...

____

____

____

____

____

2. WHAT IS THE _PRACTICE_ FOR ME FROM THE LESSON?

I am committed to doing...

____

____

____

____

3. WHAT IS MY _PRAYER_ AS A RESULT OF THE LESSON?

I am asking God to...

____

____

____

____

DAY 13

The Price of Being Me

All of my saved life, I've have fought to be me—the me that God wants me to be. I've continued this quest even when being me has subtracted people from my life and reminded me of how bad off the old me really was. You feel me?

All of us, in one way or another, struggle with being true to who God has wired us to be. My son once told me, "Dad, you have to be true to who you are." That's true, but sometimes it's easier said than done. Bernard M. Baruch has stated, "Be who you are and say what you feel, because those who mind don't matter, and those who matter don't mind." Yet, as difficult as it may be at times, any attempt to be anyone else is identity theft and fraud.

This is a truth that dreamers have to accept, and the sooner, the better. Why? Because dreamers don't just dream, they put shoe leather to their dreams. As a result, they plant one foot in the future and one foot in the now. They place an eye on heaven with a view of hell.

Dreamers are lofty in their ideas and loyal to their family and friends. They are mindful of their location, forever learning about their longings and listeners of their intuition, never allowing for laziness in their comments. Dreamers don't lie to themselves or others. Their leisure time is strategically planned, and their love is unwavering.

Of course, none of this is possible if they spend their time trying to be anyone other than the person the almighty God has wired them to be. You feel me?

I was shopping for a new camera not long ago. I wanted a full-frame Sony, and after researching and comparing prices, I laid my dollars down on the counter at Best Buy without hesitation and with complete satisfaction. I was willing to pay the price for what I wanted.

Later, I started thinking about my willingness to pay the price for my new Sony full-frame camera without hesitation and with a sense of complete satisfaction. At that very moment, I asked myself: "Where would I be today if I had to be willing without hesitation and with complete satisfaction to pay the price to be the me God wanted me to be?" You feel me?

Those of us who dream must first be willing to pay the price for being us. Any attempt to take a shortcut in this area is a recipe for long delays in the development of dreams. The late James Baldwin is one of my favorite writers, and he once wrote, "People pay for what they do, and still more for what they have allowed themselves to become. And they pay for it simply by the lives, they lead."

The price that you and I pay for being dreamers is the life we lead! That life must be authentic even when the price is painful and scarring. Jesus said, "I must do the works of Him who sent me." Ladies and Gentlemen, we can't do the works of Him who sent us without *being the him or her* He sent! John Grisham writes in *The Rainmaker*, "Don't compromise yourself—you're all you have."

There is a price for being the me that God wants me to be. There is a price for being you that God wants you to be. So, take a deep breath, and without hesitation and with complete satisfaction, place the price on the counter of today in each and every encounter you will have. It will make it easier to do the same tomorrow.

You feel me, don't you?

1. WHAT IS THE *PRINCIPLE* OF THE LESSON?
My takeaway from the lesson is...

____

____

____

____

____

____

2. WHAT IS THE _PRACTICE_ FOR ME FROM THE LESSON?
I am committed to doing…

____

____

____

____

____

3. WHAT IS MY _PRAYER_ AS A RESULT OF THE LESSON?
I am asking God to…

____

____

____

____

____

DAY 14

Traditions, Traditions, Traditions

Every people group is filled with amazing history and distinctions. Among the many things, my ancestors' voices still speak to me about is "Freedom's Eve."

Picture in your mind December 31, 1862. Across the landscape of America, African Americans are gathering together in churches and private homes. They are anxiously awaiting news concerning the Emancipation Proclamation. Would it become the law of the land or not?

At the stroke of midnight, it was January 1, 1863, and all enslaved people in the Confederate States were declared legally free! Upon hearing the news, these formerly enslaved people and even some former slave owners, prayed, shouted, and sang old "Negro Spirituals." With thanksgiving in their hearts, they fell to their knees in thanks to God and asked for safe journeys throughout various paths of the year of come.

Today, we call it "Watch Night Service." Virtually every black church will host this service or participate with other churches in "Watch Night Service." It is an amazing part of our history, distinctiveness, and tradition.

Tradition—I can't think of or say the word without being reminded of that 1971 musical "Fiddler on the Roof." Even now, I am saying to myself, "Tradition, Tradition, Tradition." What a great musical! It is filled with great songs and perhaps, even greater truths. Tevye speaks a line in the movie that serves, at least for me, as the thesis for the musical. It is: "Without our traditions, our lives would be as shaky as the fiddler on the roof."

The leadership walk becomes a tight rope walk when dealing with tradition. A leader's shelf life becomes as shaky as the fiddler on the roof. Tradition can be a great alley in moving an organization forward, or it can be an anchor in stifling progress. The challenge for every leader is to know the difference and act accordingly.

For these reasons, a leader has to be as skillful as a surgeon when dealing with tradition. Both the leader's and the organization's tone and intention depend upon it. I have known pastors that wanted to change the choir only to have the church change the pastor. I have known leaders who wanted to upgrade a company's black and white logo only to find themselves escorted to the door with a cardboard box stuffed with their belongings.

Things are no different in a leader's personal life. As individuals, we get stuck in traditions and, thus, stuck in life. A leader's traditional friends and associates are one of the most stifling aspects of this. Often, leaders fail to cultivate new, mutually beneficial, challenging relationships. To add insult to injury, there are those moments when we do, and our old friends view anyone new in our lives as a threat to them. So, as a form of appeasement, we walk away from the new. When leaders settle in this area, they push the cruise control button. As a result, rather than becoming innovators, they become curators of tradition!

Throughout my life, whenever God was ready to shift me, the gear stick was always moving toward a new relationship! As a result, I have become a better leader, father, husband, and an all-around better person. When it comes to your next shift, remember the words of Havelock Ellis, "All the art of living lies in a fine mingling of letting go and holding on."

Purpose today to allow God to boldly lead you on this tightrope walk between tradition and the new things He longs to do through you. Your leadership depends on it.

1. WHAT IS THE *PRINCIPLE* OF THE LESSON?

My takeaway from the lesson is...

____

____

____

____

____

____

2. WHAT IS THE *PRACTICE* FOR ME FROM THE LESSON?

I am committed to doing…

____

____

____

____

3. WHAT IS MY *PRAYER* AS A RESULT OF THE LESSON?

I am asking God to…

____

____

____

____

DAY 15

Until the Love Runs Out

I love what I do—and better yet, I love what I have been given the privilege of doing.

Now, I would be the first to admit that the nearly 20 years I have pastored, and the 30-plus years I have been in leadership have not been a flowerbed of ease. (You can thank my grandmother for that imagery.) However, I wouldn't subtract anything from my leadership journey now. I love doing what I do, even when the doing hurts me in some way.

The urgency of a leader's love affair with what he or she does is critical. This, more than anything else, determines how well and how long leaders do that thing they do. Yes, there are times when the work is hard—costly in every way, and there are times when it is most disheartening.

Leaders aren't good at one-night stands, they need to be in love with what they do. There are times when they become infatuated with another path or a novel idea, but those things never last, because leaders have to be in love with what they do. It's this love that keeps them creative in the midst of chaos, determined in a down market and willing also to be led while they are leading. But as long as you love it, you will continue to do it, and do it well.

As a result of this fundamental need of a leader, I can't tell you the number of times I have been asked, "What do you do after the love is gone?" Honestly, I had asked myself that question too—when something sad happened along the way, and it seemed "yesterday was all we had."

This reality and the subsequent challenge is something that every leader encounters. And a leader's ability to navigate these troubled waters takes a different set of skills. There is no doubt that breakups are hard. When I am between a rock and a hard place, I return to the truth I learned from a passage of scripture in 2 Timothy 4:7: "I have fought a good fight, I have finished my course,

I have kept the faith . . ." Whenever I felt like the love was gone, these 16 words of Paul have provided me with a breakthrough, a breakout, or a breakup.

It all begins with understanding that every leader is in a fight! Paul says, "I have fought." When the love is gone, the fight is gone. It is as simple as that. Show me a leader that no longer loves what they do, and I will show you a leader that is phoning it in. Leaders aren't interested in "faking it until they make it," they are defined by showing up and fighting for every inch of progress . . . until the love is gone. And why do they do this? Because it is a "good fight."

The first time I read this passage and completed a word study on it, I could not remain in my seat! Think about what Paul says, *I have been in a fight, but it's been a good fight.* The word "good" is *kalos* in Greek. It refers to both the intrinsic and aesthetic value in his fight. In other words, Paul says, *I love what I do so much that I fought for the privilege to do it, and I looked good fighting.* Wow!

Therefore, if you still see the intrinsic value in what you do and where you have been called to do it, throw another log on the fire of your love and fight on. You will never look better doing anything else anywhere else. So slip your gloves back on, and get back in the ring today.

Shout to the world, "I will do this until the love runs out."

1.   WHAT IS THE *PRINCIPLE* OF THE LESSON?

My takeaway from the lesson is...

____

____

____

____

____

____

2. WHAT IS THE _PRACTICE_ FOR ME FROM THE LESSON
I am committed to doing…

____

____

____

____

3. WHAT IS MY _PRAYER_ AS A RESULT OF THE LESSON?
I am asking God to…

____

____

____

____

____

DAY 16

Reinventing vs. Reinvesting

I am sure that you, as I have, have either known or heard of those we were sure would turn the world upside-down. Only to learn later that due to a series of bad decisions, the only world they turned upside down and inside-out was their own. Maybe that person is you.

For each of us, neither intellect, talent, nor riches in and of themselves shield us from the devastation of a series of bad decisions. The ruin these choices can bring upon one's life, family, career, and others that care about them can be tragic.

As a leader, no matter how honorable your intentions or pure your heart, you will make mistakes. In those instances, it's not an issue of reinventing yourself but rather the reinvesting of self that brings about a turnaround. Herein lays a leader's elasticity or flexibility.

The more public a leader may be, the more public and painful the setbacks. Leaders without this flexible disposition are more prone to burn out and burn up everyone and everything in their path rather than bouncing back. And for many, shameful and devastating failure can be especially hard when intentions are honorable and your heart is pure.

A leader's ability to regain traction after failure is sometimes a matter of finding victory somewhere else and thus reinvesting one's self in that place, rather than reinventing oneself. Marion Mill was born into wealth in Hungary. Some have reported that her first spoon was made of solid gold. Her parents, wanting nothing but the best for her, sent her to school in Vienna. There, she became an actress and fell head-over-heels for a young medical student named Otto.

The two were married and moved to Hollywood, CA. It was there that Otto became interested in making movies. This interest soon eclipsed his desire for a medical practice. He closed his practice and moved full steam ahead into making movies, becoming the internationally acclaimed director Otto Preminger.

Along the way, however, the Hollywood lifestyle became too much for his wife, Marion, and she became addicted to alcohol and drugs and was linked to numerous affairs. Her life became so twisted that Otto Preminger divorced her. After she tried to kill herself three different times, Marion moved back to Vienna.

Not long after moving back to Vienna, Marion met a well-known medical doctor named Albert Schweitzer. Not only was he a doctor, but he was a musician, philosopher, theologian, and missionary. Marion became so fascinated by Dr. Schweitzer that she met with him each week for nearly six months to discuss a host of things. When it came time for him to return to Africa, this once suicidal, alcoholic, and drug-addicted woman begged the good doctor to allow her to accompany him there. Everyone that knew them was astonished that he agreed to allow her to go.

There, in the small village of Lambaréné, Gabon, Marion reinvested herself by spending the rest of her life emptying bedpans and tearing up sheets to make bandages for putrid sores among the poverty-stricken people of Africa. There she wrote her autobiography *All I Want is Everything*. When she died, *Time Magazine* featured this quote from her autobiography: "Albert Schweitzer says there are two kinds of people. There are the helpers and the non-helpers. I thank God, He allowed me to become a helper, and in helping, I found everything."

The difference between losing everything and finding everything is reinvesting oneself in the right thing! Leaders are not made for the bench no matter how many times they have struck out. They must be at the plate or the batter's box, preparing for another swing at the ball. The distance between the batter's box and the plate is the depth of a leader's desire to help someone else. It is in reinvesting in others that a leader learns the depths of Charles Dickens's words: "No one is useless in this world that lightens the burdens of another."

This may not be a profound statement, but I guarantee you that it is profitable. If you want an additional something profound to think about, consider this: Jesus, after what some would view as a public failure, got up out of the grave . . . and what did he do? Did he reinvent himself? No! He reinvested himself. And notice, who does he reinvest himself in? The very ones that had seemingly caused his public failure! As a result of him doing this, they—as well as you and I—are the ones that are reinvented. Now that will preach!

Today is as good a day as any to reinvest yourself. Along the way, your reinvestment will also cause you to reinvent yourself, just like Marion Mill.

1. WHAT IS THE *PRINCIPLE* OF THE LESSON?

My takeaway from the lesson is...

____

____

____

____

____

____

2. WHAT IS THE PRACTICE FOR ME FROM THE LESSON?

I am committed to doing...

____

____

____

____

____

3. WHAT IS MY *PRAYER* AS A RESULT OF THE LESSON?
I am asking God to…

____

____

____

____

____

____

DAY 17

Greater! Larger!

I had just completed my last lesson in the series "Dreaming Boldly" when a man approached me and said, "I can't believe you just spent three weeks on a series about dreaming boldly when marriages in this church are falling apart." "Sir," I replied, "That is the very reason I spent three weeks teaching on dreaming. The couples you are referring to are no longer connected to their dreams."

Wiser couples, businessmen or businesswomen, pastors, or community leaders—all of can attest there was a season when we became disconnected from our dreams. Our passion for what we do has been usurped by the problems that come with doing what we do. In place of our "conquer the world" attitude, we have settled for contentment.

Aleksandr Sergeyevich Pushkin was a Russian author of the Romantic era who is considered by many to be the greatest Russian poet and the founder of modern Russian literature. He writes in one of his poems: "I've lived to bury my desires and see my dreams corrode with rust, now all that's left are fruitless fires that burn my empty heart to dust."

Allow those words to marinate for a moment. The poetic depth of his words is only matched by the depth of their sadness, and because of it, they warrant another reading: "I've lived to bury my desires and see my dreams corrode with rust, now all that's left are fruitless fires that burn my empty heart to dust."

For me, to use an idiom, "that's a bitter pile." Why? For three reasons: (1) the only desires that should be buried are those that are opposed to the will of God; (2) no matter how long we live, our dreams should not corrode with rust, leaving us with fruitless fires that burn our empty heart to dust; and (3) these 27 words reflect the state of too many people's lives today.

Our dreams shouldn't be passive pastimes. They shouldn't be limited by the border bullies of "you can't" or "you shouldn't," and they certainly should not corrode with rust, leaving us with fruitless fires that burn our empty hearts to dust.

Our dreams are important! However, many leaders have stopped dreaming, and for many, their dreams are too small.

Marko, a blogger living in Croatia, gives his observation on the subject: "It feels like no one dreams anymore. People have plans; they settle down; they have their wishes, but what happened to big dreams? What happened to generations that would change the world for the better? How many people wake up in the morning and say to themselves: 'I will change the world!'"

Sarah Farish of "Making The Most of Him 365" writes, "I don't dream big enough. Some time ago, I placed God in a box, and there He's remained . . ."

Here lies the heart of the issue: many of us have placed God in a box! Psalm 78:41 reads, "Yes, again and again, they tempted God, and limited the Holy One of Israel." The very moment leaders decide to unbox God is the very moment we reawaken His dreams for us. Paul S. Rees, in an article entitled "God in Shackles," writes these words: "It is we who put shackles upon God. We cannot keep Him from managing the stars above us, but we can prevent Him from managing the soul within us." We cannot limit God and avoid limiting our dreams.

One day Michelangelo came into the studio of Raphael and looked at one of Raphael's early drawings. He then took a piece of chalk and wrote *amplius* across the drawing, which means "greater" or "larger." Raphael's plan was too cramped and narrow.

So it is that God walks into the studio of our life and writes across its canvas *Amplius!* Greater! Larger! Our dreams are too cramped and narrow. They are limited by our problem's borders rather than our provider's resources! They are conditional because we no longer view ourselves as more than conquerors. They are comfortable rather than challenging. They are situational rather than supernatural!

While the dew still lingers in the grass and the sun tiptoes to its right place, the morning calls forth a new generation of leaders to dream. Will you answer the call? Do you hear God saying, "*Amplius!* Greater! Larger!"?

1. WHAT IS THE *PRINCIPLE* OF THE LESSON?

My takeaway from the lesson is...

____

____

____

____

____

2. WHAT IS THE *PRACTICE* FOR ME FROM THE LESSON?

I am committed to doing…

____

____

____

____

3. WHAT IS MY *PRAYER* AS A RESULT OF THE LESSON?

I am asking God to…

____

____

____

____

DAY 18

Greater Works

During the last quarter of 2012, as I do in the last part of every year, I started reflecting on my wins and losses for the year: the things I did really well, those I did not do well, and the things I did but totally flunked in.

As a result of spending much of my time either preaching or in sermon preparation, and for the last two years, sermon series planning and promoting, I naturally started grading myself in these areas. I gave myself a B in Sermon Preparation and Delivery and a C+ in Series Planning and Promoting (that was up from a D the previous year). Feeling good about my grades, I sat back with a smile on my face, and just when I was feeling really good about my success, the Holy Spirit began to deal with me concerning my overall grade in discipleship.

It didn't take more than a couple of minutes for me to sit up in my chair and hang my head low. I realized that I had flunked discipleship! I had allowed myself to define my success by the Sunday morning delivery (and everything I did in preparation for it) rather than by my daily efforts to make disciples.

I repented and asked God to show me those I could start pouring my life into more directly. He did, and I did. Truthfully, paying attention to details of discipleship has revived me. It has helped me to clarify the success of my pastorate and the success and future of the church that I lead by the glow on the faces and the growth of the men that God gave me to disciple.

Jesus looked into the faces of his disciples and said, "Greater works shall you do." This was a major part of how He defined His success. Getting those 12 men ready for his departure was a three-year strategic plan. They were to "make disciples." These men turned the world upside down because they had all of Him in all of them. This strategy was so important that Christ didn't return to heaven until his disciples completely understood they were to do for others what He had done for them.

When I look back on the grades, I gave myself in preaching, sermon series preparation, and promoting, the words of Cindy Adams rush in like a flood: "Success has made failures of many men." Our role as leaders is not defined or determined by the sermons we preach or the business we run, no matter how successful. Instead, it is defined by the servants we develop. The bravado of a sermon in and of itself is not enough to build disciples. Delivering powerful messages without deliberately developing powerful messengers is a waste of time.

The more I think about leadership, the more I am convinced that leadership is not about what a leader can give, pay, or provide for you. It is always about what a leader can pour into you; that is the heart of discipleship!

How about you? Are you passing or flunking the discipleship test? And if you are flunking, let me be the first to say you can raise your GPA. I did! And by God's grace, you can, too.

1. WHAT IS THE _PRINCIPLE_ OF THE LESSON?

My takeaway from the lesson is...

____

____

____

____

____

2. WHAT IS THE _PRACTICE_ FOR ME FROM THE LESSON?

I am committed to doing…

____

____

____

____

____

3. WHAT IS MY _PRAYER_ AS A RESULT OF THE LESSON?

I am asking God to…

____

____

____

____

____

DAY 19

One Less Problem

"Let them go" is a phrase that kept echoing from the depths of my heart. It was part of the running dialogue I had with myself. I simply couldn't decide why I was hanging on so hard.

Was it because of who it was, when it was, or how we came to this place of a different path? Honestly, I haven't completely resolved that question yet, and I have had nearly fifteen years to process it. This individual and I had agreed on virtually everything, and thus, we walked together. He had been foundational to my educational start; he filled out my college application and worked alongside me on a day laborer's job. We had drunk Kool-Aid from jelly jars together and laughed about it, and in the middle of it, we spoke prophetically to one another, saying, "It won't be like this always." Yet, after starting from the bottom and now that the whole team has moved forward in life, jelly jars and day jobs are not enough to keep us walking together.

Oh, why? Why, why had this happened? In short, I became a boss. My position was elevated, even though I, as a person, was not. It was difficult for my amigo to accept my new position. He was more comfortable with where we had been than where I was going. I still remember the day, the scene, and the scent of the room when he said, "If I have to report to you, I can't be here any longer." I responded, "You need to do what you have to do and do it quickly." With that, the fat lady sang, and the timeframe for refunds was over. It was a wrap.

As leaders, we must understand that some people are more comfortable with you being a project rather than a partner, with you being the tail rather than the head, with you living broke and busted rather than having blessings of bounty. When this happens, familiarity breeds contempt, and either you will fold from the pressure of what once was and what might have been, or you will lead!

Leadership is not like a "friends and family" cell phone plan. It doesn't become cheaper the longer you have it; it becomes more expensive. This doesn't mean that you care less about friends and family; it simply means that you are committed to leading with or without them. The closer you are to them, the more difficult this will be. Abraham had to leave his friends and family to get to what God was gifting him. Moses's brother and sister wanted the same leadership position that Moses had. Joseph's brothers didn't like him and sold him into slavery. David's brothers had problems with him too, and Jesus himself made it clear: those that weren't willing to leave father and mother, sisters and brothers, weren't worthy of Him.

Now, no matter how intense a leader desires to bring along the crew, especially when the whole team started from the bottom, if they can't handle your elevation, you must be willing to move forward in your emancipation from them. Always keep the light on for them as Paul did for Mark, but don't stop moving.

Your discomfort will probably last for no more than a short season, and the smart money is betting you'll be better off and have one less problem without them. As a leader, it's inevitable: you will be called to let people go, trusting that God will care for them. Let God show you when it is time to release others so you can keep moving forward.

1. WHAT IS THE *PRINCIPLE* OF THE LESSON?

My takeaway from the lesson is...

____

____

____

____

____

____

2. WHAT IS THE _PRACTICE_ FOR ME FROM THE LESSON?

I am committed to doing…

____

____

____

____

____

3. WHAT IS MY _PRAYER_ AS A RESULT OF THE LESSON?

I am asking God to…

____

____

____

____

____

DAY 20

Making Your Mark

President Barack Obama is quoted as saying:

Making your mark on the world is hard. If it were easy, everybody would do it. But it's not. It takes patience, it takes commitment, and it comes with plenty of failures along the way. The real test is not whether you avoid these failures because you won't. It's whether you let it harden or shame you into inaction or whether you learn from it, or whether you choose to persevere.

Persevere - There is perhaps no truer need in a leader's life than defined in this one word. This is the white-knuckle approach to the life of a leader. Every leader that has ever led anything has his or her white-knuckle story, a time when they had to move on while holding on for dear life.

In some ways, leadership has become soft today and redefined. Leadership has been reduced to million-dollar contracts for those with penniless character. Today, we celebrate victors on the field and in the sports arena while excusing the villains they are in their families and communities. Athletes have become our gods, while community leaders, pastors, and teachers have become the devil.

Just consider the degrading talking points of much of the conservative media about President Obama being a community activist before holding political office. I can almost still hear them saying, "How dare this community leader think he can lead my country. That socialist devil."

However, he persevered, and the rest is and continues to be history. Leaders must persevere the most against the onslaught of personal and professional assault. This wind blisters their faces, stalling their forward movement and pushing in direct opposition to the wind at their back. John Wesley writes in his journal:

- Sunday, A.M., May 5, preached in St. Anne's; was asked not to come back anymore.

- Sunday, P.M., May 5, Preached in St. John's. Deacons said, "Get out and stay out."
- Sunday, A.M., May 12, Preached in St. Jude's. Can't go back there, either.
- Sunday, A.M., May 19, Preached in St. Somebody Else's deacons called a special meeting and said I couldn't return.
- Sunday, P.M., May 19, Preached on street. Kicked off street.
- Sunday, A.M., May 26, Preached in meadow. Chased out of meadow as bull was turned loose during service.
- Sunday, A.M., June 2, Preached out at the edge of town. Kicked off the highway.
- Sunday, P.M., June 2, Afternoon, preached in a pasture. Ten thousand people came out to hear me.

There is always a "Wow" in me when I read and hear of leaders that have persevered against all odds. If I were a betting man, I would bet that there is a "Wow" from me in your leadership story. Why? Because you are still here! You continue to fight the good fight! You have persevered!

Leaders make their mark because they keep getting up and moving forward. They persevere! This may have been a hard week, month, day, year, or hour, but you have to keep going. Your mark in life is defined by your willingness to keep marching in life! Don't give up; your story is not yet over.

1.   WHAT IS THE _PRINCIPLE_ OF THE LESSON?

My takeaway from the lesson is...

____

____

____

____

____

2. WHAT IS THE _PRACTICE_ FOR ME FROM THE LESSON?

I am committed to doing…

____

____

____

____

____

3. WHAT IS MY _PRAYER_ AS A RESULT OF THE LESSON?

I am asking God to…

____

____

____

____

____

DAY 21

First in Jerusalem

Like most places we visit, particularly abroad, one of the first questions ask is, "Where are you from?"

This was the case as I sat on the beach of Boca Chica in Santo Domingo, Dominican Republic. The question came from a young man I later learned was from Haiti. I answered, "Indiana." He thought I said India, and before I could correct him, he said, "I didn't know there were black people in India."

The historian in me demanded that I take him on a journey first. So, in the tradition of J. A. Rogers, *From "Superman" to Man*, I started within the Horn of Africa and told him about the fruit that it has given the world; yes, even India. I watched as this young man's eyes grew, and from his entire disposition, he said, "Tell me more." Our conversation went on and on and on.

I must confess it gave me a rush to witness an awakening in this young man. He said to me, "I never heard these things before." With that one statement, I thought, "He's no different than most African-American teens living in any inner-city community in the United States.

I thought about my encounter with this young man a lot, both then and now. The expression on his face and the hunger for more knowledge still challenges me. I constantly ask myself, "How am I as a leader impacting my community?" There is an old African proverb that states, "Until the lion has his historian, the hunter will always be the hero." Every time I read or hear that statement, I think of the eminent responsibility I have in my community.

Jesus told His disciples to start in Jerusalem. That is, start where you live, where you are from and where you have connections. Start in your community. The lure of international recognition and fame has disconnected many leaders from their communities, their Jerusalem.

I was talking to an African American leader who has been very successful with an arts program. Most of the young people involved are African American children from inner-city communities. He doesn't live anywhere near it; he doesn't attend a church and doesn't have any of his programs in the community where the kids are from. I asked him one day why he wasn't doing any of his programs in the community where the children are from, commenting that surely there were buildings large enough. He responded, "I need for my kids to see something different."

Now don't get me wrong, I understand the value of exposing young inner-city children to a different environment. However, leadership that understands the "your Jerusalem" mandate also understands the need to teach them to value their community. When I suggested to him that his leadership philosophy was basically a 1960 school bussing philosophy, let's just say *he wasn't too happy about it.*

I knew this wasn't his heart's intent, but I believe it is what he was nonverbally communicating. He was saying to every kid, their parents, and their community: "I am too good to live in your community; I am too good to worship in your community; I bring no economic value to your community, but I profit from your community by taking you out of your community. I am ok with that, and you should be too."

Inner-city communities aren't in need of "The Great White Hope," even if these helpers appear in black skin. They need those who are committed to their Jerusalem in every sphere. We often forget that it was only after starting in their Jerusalem that the disciples of Jesus were able to later turn the world upside down.

The early church movement was not a move to the suburbs but to the city—the inner city. I often think about the angel coming to Phillip and telling him to go south to the desert: "And the angel of the Lord spake unto Philip, saying, Arise, and go toward the south unto the way that goeth down from Jerusalem unto Gaza, which is desert." Phillip had done very well in Samaria, but God told him to go to the "South Side" if you will allow me. What is he to do, *join* himself to the chariot of a black man? The word join means to stick like glue. The Bible says of Phillip, "So he started running until he was even with the chariot." As a result, history tells us that this Ethiopian eunuch took the gospel to Africa. Oh God, let that be you and me today.

My Haitian friend, the one I met in the Dominican Republic, thanked me for the history lesson I shared and later brought another young man from Haiti and asked me to repeat the story. I blasted from the same Horn of Africa and made two friends that day. I continued by sharing with them the Gospel of Jesus Christ. They didn't accept Christ into their hearts, but they had two seeds planted in them that day: one of education and one of eternity. When I left there and came back to my Jerusalem, I recommitted myself to doing the same.

What about you? Will you do the same in your Jerusalem?

1. WHAT IS THE *PRINCIPLE* OF THE LESSON?

My takeaway from the lesson is...

____

____

____

____

____

____

2. WHAT IS THE _PRACTICE_ FOR ME FROM THE LESSON?

I am committed to doing…

____

____

____

____

____

3. WHAT IS MY _PRAYER_ AS A RESULT OF THE LESSON?

I am asking God to…

____

____

____

____

____

DAY 22

Flex Your Flexibility

On this particular day, I stopped in on Johnny, the brother of one of my best friends, Donald. Unfortunately, Donald had died about three months earlier, and I hadn't seen any of his family since the service. Johnny welcomed me in; we sat down and traded stories about Donald, sharing how much we missed him.

I was bracing myself to get up from the chair and leave when Johnny said, "You know, Tony, I could have been dead now." This comment surprised me, so I settled back into my chair and became a captured audience.

"It was my sophomore year of college," Johnny continued, "and an altercation between me and a friend landed me against a glass cabinet, with nerves, muscles, and arteries in my right arm cut," as he raised his right arm to show me the scar, still visible 50 years later. "Tony, I laid there on the floor bleeding and thinking I was going to die. They rushed me to the hospital, and doctors stitched me up, but my baseball career was over, and I was angry."

As well as I had known the family, I had never heard this story before. I was about to ask him a question when Johnny said, "Over the next year, I had to learn to do two things: forgive my friend and learn how to do everything with my left hand. Neither one of them was easy, Tony."

Over the next hour, Johnny shared with me the difficulties of that sophomore year. I sat there amazed. I understood the need for Johnny to forgive his friend and how forgiveness was about setting both him and his friend free. However, I was in awe as he talked about learning to do everything with his left hand as a right-hander. Learning how to tie his shoes and staying up nightly pecking out his homework with one hand on a typewriter were all difficult tasks. "Tony, I refused to let someone else do it for me. I needed to do this for myself—and I did it, Tony. I graduated on time," he concluded.

Well, the time for me to leave had come, and I thought about Johnny's story on the drive home. In fact, it remains with me today. I get the forgiveness part, but as I thought about him adjusting to doing things with his left hand, leadership flexibility was all I could think about.

Strategic seasons of flexibility produce compound interest in leadership. We often miss that lesson in our Western paradigm of leadership. Ours is one of "I am the boss; I don't have to be flexible." This type of thinking and subsequent disposition produces a stubbornness and/or rigidity in our leadership style and the culture of whatever we lead. As leaders, we must keep an open attitude to new ideas and ways of doing things. There are times when we have to adjust and become comfortable with doing things with our left hand when we have only experienced doing them with our right hand.

It's important to remember that as leaders, flexing our flexibility is not an abandonment of our principles or core values. Instead, we honor both while embracing a new methodology of execution.

Years ago, Frank Lloyd Wright was given the impossible task of building the Imperial Hotel in Tokyo. No comparable construction job had ever before been undertaken. With patience, he laid plans for the immense building in this land of earthquakes and terrible tremors. After carefully reviewing the situation, he found that eight feet below the surface of the ground lay a 60-foot bed of soft mud. Why not float the great structure on this and in some way make it absorb the shock of the earthquake?

After four years of work, amid ridicule and jeers of skeptical onlookers, this most difficult building in the world was completed. Soon after its completion, the day arrived that tested the structure completely. The worst earthquake in 52 years caused houses and buildings all around to tumble and fall in ruins. But the Imperial Hotel stood! Because it could adjust itself to the earth's tremors, it stood tall. [1]

In truth, the mud gave the building the flexibility it needed. Allow that to soak in for a moment. The mud gave the building the flexibility it needed. Life and

---

[1] A. Smith, in Resources, #2.

leadership obstacles can be lessons in how to flex our flexibility. It is often within the muddiest situations that leaders learn flexibility, to let go, loosen up and let God. This is what Johnny reminded me of that day.

Oh, by the way, The Imperial Hotel in Tokyo was completed in 1923 and stood until 1968. The building was demolished to make room for new construction because of its flexibility.

1. WHAT IS THE _PRINCIPLE_ OF THE LESSON?

My takeaway from the lesson is...

____

____

____

____

____

2. WHAT IS THE _PRACTICE_ FOR ME FROM THE LESSON?

I am committed to doing...

____

____

____

____

____

____

____

____

3. WHAT IS MY _PRAYER_ AS A RESULT OF THE LESSON?

I am asking God to…

____

____

____

____

____

____

DAY 23

I Feel Like a Failure

I feel like a failure, he said, his words traveling through the phone line and into my ear. These were words from a dear friend who gave his heart to what he believed God had called him to do. Now he was on the verge of losing everything, including his money.

But the idea that others would view this as an indictment of his integrity bothered him the most. This thought actually gave him nightmares. A shift in the housing market had caused a shift in how others viewed him. Those that once sang his praises were now calling for his head, even though they knew he had done nothing wrong. Nothing!

I knew this young man and was well acquainted with the situation, so my goal was to lend an ear. All leaders need someone to lend them an ear, in general—and particularly when the tides have turned. His spirit was down. His head was down. And if there is one thing that I have learned throughout my leadership life is that one of the most difficult things leaders have to do is discover one reason to hold their head up when there are 1,000 reasons to hold their head down.

The more public a leader's failure becomes, the more tempting it becomes for one to view themselves as a failure. Leaders instinctively marry themselves to the event of failure, and in many instances, they get locked into a death-do-us-part situation. Rather than growing through a situation, they die from it.

As hard as it may be, leaders must divorce themselves from failure. They must not allow it to define them. No matter what others' opinions may be, we must never view ourselves as a failure. We must find a way to get back into the game.

On New Year's Day, 1929, a crowd of 70,000 gathered to watch Georgia Tech play the University of California in the Rose Bowl. In that game, a man named

Roy Riegels recovered a fumble for California. Somehow, he became confused and started running 65 yards in the wrong direction. One of his teammates, Benny Lom, outdistanced and downed him just before scoring for the opposing team. When California attempted to punt, Tech blocked the kick and scored a safety which was the ultimate margin of victory.

That strange play came in the first half of the game, and everyone who was watching was asking the same question: "What will Coach Nibbs Price do with Roy Riegels in the second half?" The men filed off the field and went into the locker room. They sat down on the benches and on the floor, all but Riegels. He put his blanket around his shoulders, sat down in a corner, put his face in his hands, and cried like a baby.

If you have played football, you know that a coach usually has a great deal to say to his team during halftime. That day, Coach Price was quiet. No doubt he was trying to decide what to do with Riegels. Then the timekeeper came in and announced there were three minutes left before playing time.

Coach Price looked up at the team and said, "Men, the same team that played the first half will start the second." The players got up and started out, all but Riegels. He did not budge. The coach looked back and called to him again; still, he didn't move. Coach Price went over to where Riegels sat and said, "Roy, didn't you hear me? The same team that played the first half will start the second." Then Roy Riegels looked up, and his cheeks were wet with a strong man's tears.

"Coach," he said, "I can't do it to save my life. I've ruined you, I've ruined the University of California, and I've ruined myself. I couldn't face that crowd in the stadium to save my life."

Then Coach Price reached out, put his hand on Riegel's shoulder, and said, "Roy, get up and go on back; the game is only half over." And Roy Riegels went back, and those Tech men will tell you that they have never seen a man play football as Roy Riegels played that second half.[2]

My words to you today are the same words I gave my friend who felt like a failure. "The game is not over. Get up, get back in it and play like your life depended upon it!" My friend did, and you can too! The time to start again is now.

1. WHAT IS THE _PRINCIPLE_ OF THE LESSON?

My takeaway from the lesson is...

____

____

____

____

____

[2] Haddon W. Robinson, Christian Medical Society Journal

2. WHAT IS THE _PRACTICE_ FOR ME FROM THE LESSON?
I am committed to doing…

____

____

____

____

____

3. WHAT IS MY _PRAYER_ AS A RESULT OF THE LESSON?
I am asking God to…

____

____

____

____

____

DAY 24

Not Many Fathers

A funny thing happened to me on my way to my airplane seat. It had been a restful ten days in Santo Domingo, and I was looking forward to going home. I upgraded my seat for more legroom, and as I approached my seat, I saw there was a gentleman already sitting there.

Now, I have been saved for a long time, so I won't even begin to share with you the thoughts that were going through my mind. I said to him, "4C," and before I could finish my sentence he said, "Is this your seat?" "Yes," I responded. Then he said, "I have a first-class ticket and will switch my seat for yours." Now I really was speechless. "Ah, okay," I struggled to say, not wanting to appear too excited.

As we switched tickets, I glanced at the man sitting next to him; he looked like he could have been the man's father. As I turned to go to first class I said to myself, "I bet he wanted to sit next to his father." Yet even as I got myself situated in my first-class seat; I began to struggle emotionally without knowing why. I should have been happy, but I wasn't.

Then it hit me! I started to think about all the places I've been and the cities and countries I've seen. I've traveled with my mother, wife, children, grandmother, and many others—but never with my father. With that single thought, it was as if someone had taken an eraser to the places I had been and erased all the things I had done. As I mentally and emotionally attempted to rewrite the lines of those memories, I fought back tears. Jacob wrestled with the angel for a blessing and was left limping; I, on the other hand, was left without my father's blessing.

I thought I was over this, was the sermon I kept preaching to myself as I sat in my seat. *I am 55 years old, and I should not be dealing with this. Here I am, a successful man by human standards, and very successful by God's standards, and I am fighting back tears over a man that at worst didn't love me or at best didn't know how. Either way, I can't afford this right now.*

I wrestled for peace, but it wasn't forthcoming. "What am I to do?" I asked myself. I am a black man sitting in first class, and I can't even enjoy it. I cannot be crying over this!"

At that moment, the flight attendant broke into my thoughts. "Would you like some lunch, sir?" "Sir?" I repeated to myself; they don't call you that in coach. "What are the lunch options?" I asked. "Turkey sandwich or salad," she replied. I responded, "I'll have the turkey." No sooner had she turned and walked away than I picked up my last train of thought and continued to preach: *I wish getting over this was as simple as ordering a turkey sandwich.*

The fact is, there is nothing simple about getting over father issues, whether you're male or female. My own personal struggles reminded me of that. Over the process of time, I have reflected upon that plane ride and asked myself repeatedly, "Does my leadership style have anything to do with the absence of my father in my life?" The clear answer for me is *yes*, at least today.

I know that I have held on to employees that I should have fired a long time ago because of—dare I say it—my father's issues. However, it hasn't been all bad. In many instances, holding on that extra time has been just what the person needed to turn it around.

Paul writes in 1 Corinthians 4:15, "Even if you had ten thousand guardians in Christ, you do not have many fathers, for in Christ Jesus I became your father through the gospel." This suggests to me that at the core of leadership development is a fathering component. More often than not, the reflection in the mirror of our leadership style is the reflection of our father and our desire to be or not to be him. Your future as a leader doesn't have to be limited by whether or not you have a good father in your life. Nor do your dreams have to be limited by the dreams that your father had for your life, no matter how good of a father he was or is. However, one thing is certain, fathering is vital to leadership development.

Well, my journey of tears ended after my three-hour flight back to the States. After we landed in Atlanta, I was making my way to customs when I had the opportunity to ask the man who had given me his first-class seat if that was his father seated next to him. He responded, "Yes." I replied: "Then you had the better seat." We are wise when we recognize the impact fathering has had on our leadership journey.

1. WHAT IS THE *PRINCIPLE* OF THE LESSON?

My takeaway from the lesson is...

____

____

____

____

____

2. WHAT IS THE *PRACTICE* FOR ME FROM THE LESSON?

I am committed to doing…

____

____

____

____

____

3. WHAT IS MY *PRAYER* AS A RESULT OF THE LESSON?

I am asking God to…

____

____

DAY 25

Winning by Losing

"Dad, they left us," are the words that maneuvered through the phone line and into my ear and heart.

These four words came from my then 15-year-old daughter. Lydia's short statement was no small matter. The leaders of the field trip that she and her best friend were on with another church had driven off without them, leaving two 15-year-old girls at a water park three hours away from home. To say the least, I was furious at the church leaders and fearful for the girls. However, I had to keep calm for the girls' sake. I could sense Lydia's fear, and I could hear Kristina in the background asking, "What are we going to do?"

"I will phone the church," I said to Lydia, "and they will have the bus return. I love you, and everything is going to be alright." I hung up and phoned the church. As I waited for someone to answer, I prayed, *God, don't let anything happen to these girls. Please, please, God, protect them*, even as I wept.

As I phoned the church, it seemed like hours before someone answered. During the delay, all the horror stories from my years as a counselor flooded my mind. In those moments, every sexually abused child, teenager, and adult that was on my case load or whose case had been staffed with me were represented in the present state of Lydia and Kristina. I was helpless and three hours away. God what do I say to my wife? What do I say to Kristina's mother and grandparents?

As my thoughts and emotions raced, I was suddenly interrupted by a "hello" from the other end of the phone. "Yes, this is Pastor Payton, and my daughter and her best friend are on a bus trip with your church and the bus has left them at the park," I said. "Yes, we are aware of it, the youth leader said he didn't have time to go back and get them. They have a dinner appointment in Chicago for the others on the trip, and they don't want to be late. I am sorry that I have to repeat this to you," were the words of the lady at the other end of the call.

At this point, I didn't feel very much like a pastor, a Christian or a leader. The only thing I was reflecting on was getting my hands on this youth leader. I hung up the phone, told my wife what had just happened, what was said, and that I was going to get the girls. I broke every speed limit, made it to the park, picked up the girls and made it back to the church at about the same time the bus was returning. I was beyond mad!

To make matters worse, the youth leader didn't think he had done anything wrong. The Pastor was cold and didn't think this was important enough to come off of his sabbatical, even though he was in town. A local television station called me for a statement, and a lawyer from Kristina's mother's attorney phoned me from New York and wanted to know if I was going to join them in the lawsuit. All of this happened within 24 hours. I refused to comment to the media and told the lawyer that I was not comfortable with suing a church but that I needed to talk to someone.

I set up a meeting with Pastor Jesse White and shared everything with him. He responded, "Payton, you have a case, but that is a church, and you have to live here. I don't believe that God wants this. He protected the girls, and He wants you to protect His church." I knew he was right. I phoned the lawyer in New York and told him that I was not going to be joining in the lawsuit and would make every effort to convince Kristina's mother and grandparents not to sue the church.

Then I met with the grandparents and talked to Kristina's mother by phone. They decided not to sue. In the years that have followed, the membership of the church involved has outgrown my own and that of many others in the community, and the congregation has become more diverse.

Just the other day I was driving into the parking lot of my church and noticed a man that had been on my case load about 20 years ago. I stopped and said hello, he introduced me to his daughter and said, "I wished I had listened to you 20 years ago, but I finally got my life together. I have been off drugs for four years now and I am a member of…" And he called the church's name.

After I commended him on his progress, we shook hands, he said "thank you," and I went into my office. When I put my key into the door, I could hear Pastor White saying, "Payton you have to live here."

Leadership is often less about what leaders have the right to do and more about what is right to do. I sat down in my office chair and wept at the thought that a single life had been changed through the life of this church, probably because I refused to bring shame on said church. Jesus had the right to call a legion of angels to his aid, but he refused to. Great leaders always have the right people in their life to remind them of this. Do you?

1. WHAT IS THE *PRINCIPLE* OF THE LESSON?

My takeaway from the lesson is...

____

____

____

____

____

2. WHAT IS THE *PRACTICE* FOR ME FROM THE LESSON?

I am committed to doing…

____

____

____

____

____

____

3. WHAT IS MY _PRAYER_ AS A RESULT OF THE LESSON?
I am asking God to…

____

____

____

____

____

____

DAY 26

Daughters in Leadership

I didn't know what to expect from the meeting.

Our last conversation had not gone well. Now about six months had passed, and I would have been content to put off talking for another six months. However, her husband had texted me and requested the meeting. Even though we had parted ways, I still respected him, and God wouldn't have it any other way.

She arrived on time but with no husband in hand. This added to my nervousness about the meeting. I whispered a prayer to God in my heart and invited her in. She was as nervous about the meeting as I was. We were polite to one another, complimented each other on how well the other was looking. And with the last word of a polite introduction, an awkward silence filled the room for what seemed like hours.

As we both stumbled with what to say next, Debbie broke the silence and began to share her heart. She started out by sharing with me the state of mind she was in all those months ago and why she had said and done certain things. In the midst of this, she shifted gears and said something that rocked my world and caused me to fight back tears. Debbie continued, "I never had a relationship with my father. Our relationship was the closest thing that I had to a father/daughter relationship. When it ended, I went through the stages of grief but I stayed at the stage of anger. I felt like my daddy had abandoned me." I melted. I said to myself and to Debbie, "I am sorry."

I missed it. What I had missed is what men have a tendency to miss when it comes to developing women leaders— particularly in ministry: the powerful dynamics of the father/daughter relationship. I wounded Debbie, not because of the facts, but because I didn't father her. She expected me to correct her but she did not expect me to turn cold toward her.

The responsibility male leadership has in developing women leaders is one of validation. Women's development as leaders is built on this foundation. When male leadership misses this, they create a space of vulnerability in women; and the more desperate a woman is, the more vulnerable she is to succumb to wolves.

The reality of fatherlessness in the lives of daughters, particularly in inner cities, demands that men lead in this context. We need to fill the vacuum by validating those women that serve alongside of us and live and dream among us. We need female leaders just as much as we need male leaders.

Remember that God used both Mordecai's and Esther's leadership to save a nation. Both of them were indispensable to God's plan. Along the way, it is interesting to notice that Mordecai helped to raise up Esther, serving as a father figure in her life.

After my meeting with Debbie, I texted my biological daughter and said, "If I haven't told you lately, I love you and am proud of you." I phoned a young lady that has become a daughter to Sandy and I and left a message on her phone, "I know that it's been hard completing your education and raising a son as a single parent, but I wanted you to know that we love you and are proud of you. I know you will complete this PhD program and go on to bigger and better things. No matter how hard it gets, know that you are loved."

Both young women responded in their own way. It was what they needed to hear that day. May we keep our hearts open to raising up many more women in leadership, many more women like Esther: daughters with a purpose.

1. WHAT IS THE *PRINCIPLE* OF THE LESSON?
My takeaway from the lesson is...

____

____

____

____

____

____

____

2. WHAT IS THE _PRACTICE_ FOR ME FROM THE LESSON?

I am committed to doing…

____

____

____

____

3. WHAT IS MY _PRAYER_ AS A RESULT OF THE LESSON?

I am asking God to…

____

____

____

____

____

DAY 27

Rumba, Young Man, Rumba

Name one leader you admire. Then I will show you a leader who has been ambushed and attacked on every side. It comes with the territory of leadership; it is a given.

Albert Pike is quoted as saying, "He who endeavors to serve, to benefit and improve the world, is like a swimmer, who struggles against a rapid current, in a river lashed into angry waves by the winds. Often, they roar over his head, often they beat him back and baffle him."

Leadership is no walk in the park. It often resembles the dance of a cat on a hot tin roof. It's a fight. Those that lead often struggle against a rapid current. Nevertheless, we are called to make a difference in this world. In the words of that old African American song, we "have a charge to keep and a God to glorify."

So how do we accomplish this? We start by never losing sight of the significance of our role in divine change. Put simply, there is value in the role you play in God's divine plan. He knows the plans He has for you. You are here to impact time for eternity.

The Apostle Paul puts it this way:

We are cracked and chipped from our afflictions on all sides, but we are not crushed by them. We are bewildered at times, but we do not give in to despair. We are persecuted, but we have not been abandoned. We have been knocked down, but we are not destroyed.

(2 Corinthians 4:8-12 The Voice)

After watching the US team lose in the World Cup today, I was reminded of how close they came to victory a few days ago . . . within seconds! Likewise, we can spend all our time, passion, and energy fighting for victory in any area of our lives and be within seconds of obtaining victory, only to have the enemy come in at the last second and snatch it away from us!

There truly is no "downtime" in our lives. Every day is a battle. Remember, it was during David's rest period that he decided to take a stroll on the roof and laid eyes on Bathsheba. And we all know how that ended.

In the 1980s, there was a police drama on television called Hill Street Blues. Each morning the duty officer would give out assignments concerning the areas that needed continued patrolling and cases that were still open with things that still needed to be done. Each morning he would close the briefings by saying, "Be careful out there."

For each of us, there are areas in our lives that need continued patrolling and cases that are still open with things that still need to be done. Let us do our job. Let us continue to do the work of the ministry. Let us continue with our reasonable service. But along the way, *be careful out there.*

You are here for a reason and a season, to impact time for eternity. Please remember there is always a "Rising From The Dust" for all of us. Therefore, "Rumba, young man (or woman), Rumba."

1. WHAT IS THE *PRINCIPLE* OF THE LESSON?

My takeaway from the lesson is...

____

____

____

____

____

2. WHAT IS THE _PRACTICE_ FOR ME FROM THE LESSON?

I am committed to doing…

____

____

____

____

____

3. WHAT IS MY _PRAYER_ AS A RESULT OF THE LESSON?

I am asking God to…

____

____

____

____

____

DAY 28

Take Someone with You

A few days ago, I was invited to a meeting with Congressman Marlin Stutzman. The meeting was to be attended by a group of pastors—particularly African American pastors from Fort Wayne, Indiana. And quite frankly, I rarely attend a political meeting. However, I said yes to this one because of the respect that I have for the person who asked me to attend.

The morning of the meeting came and I honestly had forgotten about it. About an hour before the meeting, the text came from Roger, reminding me. I responded, "Yes, I will be there," rushing to get dressed. I recall saying to myself, "Man, I am glad that Roger's office is close." After getting dressed and running out of the door, I suddenly felt the nudging of the Spirit to invite my son to go to the meeting with me. He was visiting home from Fort Lauderdale, Florida and was still in the bed.

I rushed back in the house, knocked on his bedroom door and said, "I have to go to a meeting and I want you to go with me. Get up, put some nice clothes on and meet me downstairs." He did all that I asked, and off to the meeting we went. We arrived early, so I had an opportunity to introduce him to both Roger and Mark. They laughed and joked with him about coming to Fort Wayne in November from Florida. Mark, a very successful businessman and awesome leader asked, "What brings you home?" Zachary responded, "I think God is calling me home to help my father."

I thought Mark was going to jump out of his chair. He looked at me and looked back a Zachary and said, "That's great! You know why that's great because your dad can trust you."

About that time, Congressman Stutzman arrived. We made our way to the board room, and I introduced my son to him and many of those in the room. Some knew who he was, shook his hand, hugged him, and talked about how good it was to see him. As we sat down, just before the meeting started, Mark made his way back to Zachary and gave him his card and said, "If you need anything, call me. I think it is wonderful that you are considering coming home to help your dad, and anything I can do to help, I will."

The meeting finally began, and Congressman Stutzman shared his heart on an array of issues facing our community and country. It was a great meeting. However, my mind keeps drifting back to the way my son was received by everyone at the meeting. I took a mental snapshot of the smile on his face as people greeted him and asked about him. It was a smile that I hadn't seen in a while, one that I will never forget and one that I pray will never depart from his face.

The meeting ended. Mark came over to Zachary and reminded him to call him if he needed anything, shook his hand and said goodbye. Zachary and I got in the car and made our way back home. He asked me about Mark. Of all the great leaders in room that day, the one that impressed him the most was Mark. A 70+-year-old short white man had impressed and impacted a 26-year-old, 6'6" African American man. I am very sure they don't have the same playlist or reading list. Their background is different, and dare I say it, the color of their skin is different—but given all of that, Mark impressed and impacted my son.

There are two things that great leaders do. First, they add value to people, and secondly, they do so by being themselves. No one will ever be a great leader without being himself or herself. Leaders impress and impact because they are true to who they are, and they value the true you.

In his book *Secrets of the Millionaire Mind*, T. Harv Eker writes:

Your life is not just about you. It's also about contributing to others. It's about living true to your mission and reason for being here on this earth at this time. It's about adding your piece of the puzzle to the world. Most people are so stuck in their egos that everything revolves around me, me, and more me. But if you want to be rich in the truest sense of the word, it can't only be about you. It has to include adding value to other people's lives.

Thank you, Mark, for being a great leader and adding value to my son. How will you "take someone with you" today?

1. WHAT IS THE _PRINCIPLE_ OF THE LESSON?

My takeaway from the lesson is...

2. WHAT IS THE _PRACTICE_ FOR ME FROM THE LESSON?

I am committed to doing...

3. WHAT IS MY _PRAYER_ AS A RESULT OF THE LESSON?

I am asking God to...

DAY 29

Unsung Leaders

Tinker Hatfield was a track-and-field athlete at the University of Oregon. He was such an outstanding athlete that he entered the university on a track-and-field scholarship and held the school's pole-vaulting record for a while.

Tinker had a teammate who was none other than the renowned Steve Prefontaine, one of the most celebrated track stars in the history of the sport. Needless to say, because of Steve's stardom, Tinker didn't get much attention. He was OK with that, however; his passion was architecture.

About four years after graduation, Tinker was floundering in a corporate architecture job. Bill Bowerman, his former track coach, called him. Bowerman had helped start a company that was beginning to flourish and they needed help designing marketing materials. So, in 1980, Bowerman hired Tinker on a part-time basis and started him working on an internal marketing manual. A year later, the position grew into a full-time position. This led to Tinker working on showrooms, offices and retail-space concepts: the kinds of things that ultimately mattered much less than the way whole buildings were designed.

Then in 1985, Tinker was asked to compete in a company-wide design contest. He was excited and took the opportunity seriously. As a result, Tinker's designs were so radical that many of his coworkers thought he should be fired. However, Tinker didn't care. Tinker didn't win the contest that year, but at least he gave them something to talk about.

As time went by, two of the company's top executives suddenly walked out. They were going to start their own company, and the biggest client the company had was likely to go with them. As a result, Tinker was challenged to come up with a design that would keep their most important client and save the company. He researched and worked. He started designs and trashed them. But finally, the day came. Everything was riding on this man that had spent much of his time in the shadows.

Truthfully, this was the biggest presentation of Tinker's life. The meeting was scheduled, but the client came in four hours late. It was clear that the client had made up his mind; he was planning to leave the company. "All right, show me what you got," the client grumbled. Then Tinker pulled a black cover off of the design in the center of the table. The client grabbed it smiling. He hadn't seen the new logo, and he loved it! He looked at it from every angle and couldn't put it down.

Because of Tinker's work, the client agreed to stay with the company, and in February 1988, the Air Jordan III hit the shelves. The shoes sold for $100 a pair. And Michael Jordan, the client, wore the shoe with the "jump man" logo in the 1988 NBA Slam Dunk Contest, winning it. Later, Spike Lee directed Mars Blackmon spots, featuring himself as Blackmon who famously says, "It's gotta be the shoes!"

Tinker Hatfield was an unsung leader. He worked in the background, but his impact was and continues to be felt on the frontline. Every business, church, every for-profit and not-for-profit organization, depends on those leaders that show up day after day and work behind the scenes. They add value to lives as well as to the bottom line. They are not looking for the stage, nor are they reaching for the mic. They have what Dr. Martin Luther King referred to as "the drum major" mentality.

Perhaps that's you today. You have no desire for the spotlight, but you would like to hear someone say "thank you" occasionally. I say thank you! Thank you for typing letters, making copies, cleaning the building and preparing lunches. Thank you for smiling when those of us in the spotlight have given you every reason to frown. Thank you for saying "yes" to last minute requests. Thank you for working for much less than you are worth and accepting a pay cut when the budget gets tight.

Your commitment makes the spotlight possible for those of us that get to stand in it. You may be unsung, but you definitely are not an underachiever.

1. WHAT IS THE _PRINCIPLE_ OF THE LESSON?
My takeaway from the lesson is...

____

____

____

____

____

____

2. WHAT IS THE _PRACTICE_ FOR ME FROM THE LESSON?
I am committed to doing…

____

____

____

____

____

____

3. WHAT IS MY _PRAYER_ AS A RESULT OF THE LESSON?
I am asking God to…

____

____

____

____

DAY 30

A Good Cry

Among the many books that occupy my library, Tom Lutz's *Crying: The Natural and Cultural History of Tears*, is one of the most interesting. Being a history buff, the idea of a "Cultural History of Tears" spoke to me. There are many fascinating aspects of this book; however, I offer you this quote from the book:

. . . Throughout human history, some tears have been considered good and some, like those that are not "genuine," have been held in contempt. Some tears do honor to human nature, some debase it . . . But while it is fair to say that the "good cry" and the debased cry have always been with us and always will be, what constitutes a good cry changes over time.

According to Lutz, what defines a good cry changes over time. Yet, it is my belief that everyone knows when they have had a good cry—yet few know when they are in need of one. Leadership can be a journey of triumphs, but it can also be a journey of tears. And sometimes a leader's best friend is a good cry.

Traditionally, leaders that express tears have been regarded as weak. This is especially true with male leaders. For women leaders, their entire leadership position might be undermined with the show of tears.

Now, I am not suggesting crying as a leadership strategy, but I am suggesting that every leader should be attached to a cause that is worth tolerating some occasional tears. The shortest verse in the Bible says, "Jesus wept." Sarah Watson, who serves as Chief Strategy Officer of BBH New York, is quoted as saying: "Leadership in particular is about making an authentic stand that others relate to. And crying could be a powerful part of this, at the right moment."

My friend Yolanda Walker helped me in the editing process of the book, and after reading some pages, she texted me the following message. "You have the best stories ever! Amazing! Love it! You weep a lot too, LOL." I mused on this myself, and later I started to think about her words, "You weep a lot too." I hadn't thought about it before, but she was right. It reminded me of how far I had journeyed.

In the past, I spent so much of my life being frozen emotionally. My former lifestyle did not allow tears, but now they flow for the right cause and the right call.

It is also true that in today's culture of leadership, tears are costly. Vulnerability is the price that leaders pay for their tears. What makes this price easier to pay is the cause attached to the tears. Jeremiah is referred to as the weeping prophet—this is because he spent so much of his ministry crying for and over the people God had forewarned him about, those who would not listen to him.

Leaders must be committed to something that warrants a good cry. There has to be an emotional attachment as well as an intellectual attachment to the things we do and the causes that we take up. It is a chilling and worrisome sign that weeping in babies is viewed as a sign of health and evidence of life, yet it is viewed as a weakness in those of us who are called to lead people into abundant life.

Harlan Ellison once remarked, "Like the wind crying endlessly through the universe, time carries away the names and the deeds of conquerors and commoners alike. And all that we are, all that remains, is in the memories of those who cared we came this way for a brief moment."

Think about those words and the work that you have been called to do. And then go ahead in good faith. Give yourself permission to have a good cry.

1. WHAT IS THE _PRINCIPLE_ OF THE LESSON?
My takeaway from the lesson is...

____

____

____

____

____

____

2. WHAT IS THE _PRACTICE_ FOR ME FROM THE LESSON?

I am committed to doing…

____

____

____

____

3. WHAT IS MY _PRAYER_ AS A RESULT OF THE LESSON?

I am asking God to…

____

____

____

____

DAY 31

A Best Buy I Couldn't Pass By

Once, while vacationing in Myrtle Beach, I found a Best Buy store. That's not a surprise for those that know me.

I made sure that I went everywhere my wife wanted to go first, and then, three days into the vacation, I asked her if she would allow me to go to Best Buy. Yes, I did say *allow* me. If you are a man and have been married more than two weeks, you know what I am talking about. Sandy gave me that *What you talking about, Willis?* look, but I had played my hand well. Since I had gone everywhere she wanted to go first, she said yes. I felt like a kid whose mommy had given him permission to go outside and play *before* homework.

We drove about 20 minutes to the closest store since I didn't want to press my luck. I got out of the car and walked in with the disposition of the dog in the "Kibbles 'n Bits" commercial and took a straight line to the electronic section of the store.

A young man greeted me, asking, "How can I help you, sir?" "I'm looking for the new Sony a7 full frame camera," I responded. "This way, sir. I see you know your cameras." After going over the specs with me (which I pretended I didn't already know), he suddenly started talking about how important God was in his life. I thought this was unusual. I hadn't said anything to him about God or faith. *Was he attempting to witness to me?* I thought.

OK. I'm going to roll with this and take this conversation deeper. I asked, "What is your faith?" He responded quickly: "Baptist." "So you are a Christian," I continued, and he said, "Yes." Most people would have stopped at this point and said something like, "I am, too." But I have learned that being a Christian means different things to different people, so I continued my investigation.

I asked the young man why he was Baptist and not another denomination. He said, "I think it has something to do with the teaching of John the Baptist." I said to myself, *Houston, we have a problem.* "OK," I responded and continued with, "Why are you a Christian, and not, let's say, Muslim?"

I wish I could say that I was surprised with his answer, but I wasn't. He said, "There is no difference between Christianity and Islam. They are the same book basically. I studied Islam for three years, and my girlfriend is Muslim. So we read both the Bible and Qur'an and talk about how there is basically no difference."

I continued to shop and he continued to help me. Then he was pulled away to help another customer. Later he returned to help me. I made my purchase. I began to explain to him the difference between Christ and other religions. He gave me his full attention, and the Holy Spirit talked! When God finished, the young man hugged me in the middle of the camera section of Best Buy. (Now that surprised me.) Then he said something that I will always remember: "God sent you in here! Thank you so much."

As I walked out of the store with a new tool in hand, I was reminded of the burden in my heart. The day before we left for vacation, I received a legal letter about some very troubling news. For five days, I carried the weight of the letter because I wanted my wife to enjoy the vacation she so deserved.

However, as we were away, I continued to ponder, pray and petition God for help with this matter. His answer to me was the trip to Best Buy that I now realize was more about a mission than merchandise. It was more about the context of a young man's belief in Christ than a new camera for me.

There are lots of things that I have attempted to do in my life: to pastor, to teach, to be a loving husband, to be a compassionate father and grandfather. All of those and many more are honorable. However, there is nothing like watching God using you to lead someone to Christ or lead someone to a deeper knowledge of Christ. There is no greater honor in leadership than knowing you are being led to lead in this context.

As I thought about my encounter with the young man in Best Buy, I concluded that if God was willing to arrange things in my life so that I would have the honor to share with this young man, he could likewise arrange things to halt all legal action in its tracks.

What does God want to do or to speak through you on this day? He has made my life and ministry worthwhile. And He will be faithful to lead you into the leadership and ministry opportunities He has for you, even in the middle of a Best Buy store. Watch for Him to move and speak through you today.

1. WHAT IS THE *PRINCIPLE* OF THE LESSON?
My takeaway from the lesson is...

____

____

____

____

____

____

2. WHAT IS THE *PRACTICE* FOR ME FROM THE LESSON?
I am committed to doing…

____

____

____

____

____

3. WHAT IS MY _PRAYER_ AS A RESULT OF THE LESSON?

I am asking God to…

____

____

____

____

____

DAY 32

Swagger and Sweat

swag·ger / verb; to walk or behave in a very confident way

Civilizations of old, such as the Greeks, valued physical and mental exertion. Today, ours is an environment that has made it easy to live fundamentally lazy and slothful lives.

Virtually every new invention of science and technology is about making our lives easier. These so-called time-, energy- and money-saving tools have reduced exertion of movement (aside from the movement of our thumbs).

Just think, not long from now, we will probably be able to stand in a mirror and watch the pounds melt away, while someone else on a treadmill in another country is exerting the energy to make it happen! This reminds me of the story about a man who went to his doctor and asked for a certificate for time off work. His doctor said, "You're just plain lazy." The man replied, "Sure, but give me a medical name, because I have to report back to my wife."

The truth is, laziness is not an infirmity; it is a sin! Furthermore, leadership and laziness don't even belong in the same room together. The very idea of a lazy leader is a misnomer. It's not a freak of nature; it's a freak of our own creation! Laziness should be as far removed from leadership as heaven is from the earth, as East is from West. Yet, there are those that act as if leadership is a matter of style or as young people say, *swagger*. Leadership is about movement. It's about the exertion of energy for a call and cause. That energy should be exerted physically, but also mentally, socially, and spiritually. Even a leader's rest is for the purpose of reenergizing.

Leading people to a place of realizing their dreams and destiny has less to do with scoring style points and more to do with drops of sweat. A leader's style may make it look easy from the outside, but ask any leader that has accomplished anything, and he or she will shout from the rooftops: "I worked my butt off to get here!" That which forms this type of leader is the pleasure gained in doing the work.

Nineteen years ago, when I accepted the pastoral position at Come As You Are Community Church, they could only pay me $25 a week. I had a wife and two children, and I still took the job, even though I had a better paying job at the time. I worked just as hard for that $25 as I had worked for the nearly $500 a week. Why? There was a cause; I was called to attend to it; and I felt good doing it.

Nineteen years later I still feel-good doing what I do. The work was and continues to be hard, but the pleasure I get from doing it outweighs the hard work! That pleasure is not gained by the amount of digits on a paycheck.

When the company founded by Andrew Carnegie was taken over by the US Steel Corporation in 1901, it acquired as one of its obligations a contract to pay the top Carnegie executive, Charles M. Schwab, the then unheard-of minimum sum of one million dollars. J.P. Morgan of US Steel was in a quandary about it. The highest salary on record then was one hundred thousand dollars. He met with Schwab, showed him the contract, and hesitantly asked what could be done about it.

"This," said Schwab, as he took the contract and tore it up. That contract had paid Schwab one thousand, three hundred dollars the year before. "I didn't care what salary they paid me," Schwab later told a *Forbes Magazine* interviewer. He continued:

I was not animated by money motives. I believed in what I was trying to do, and I wanted to see it brought about. I cancelled that contract without a moment's hesitation. Why do I work? I work for just the pleasure I find in work, the satisfaction there is in developing things, in creating. Also, the associations business begets. The person who does not work for the love of work, but only for money, is not likely to make money or to find much fun in life.[3]

---

[3] Bits and Pieces, May 1991, p.

Yes, a leader must employ sweat and swagger. The sweat comes from the amount of *work you put in your hours*, not the hours you put in your work. And the swagger comes from the pure pleasure you get from doing you.

1. WHAT IS THE _PRINCIPLE_ OF THE LESSON?
My takeaway from the lesson is...

____

____

____

____

____

____

2. WHAT IS THE _PRACTICE_ FOR ME FROM THE LESSON?
I am committed to doing…

____

____

____

____

____

3. WHAT IS MY _PRAYER_ AS A RESULT OF THE LESSON?

I am asking God to…

____

____

____

____

____

DAY 33

Leadership Decision

For 19 years, I have been the Pastor of Come As You Are Community Church. Before that, I served in many different leadership positions and in many different organizations. God has graced me with the opportunity to serve under and alongside many that I consider great leaders. I have studied the subject of leadership almost as much as I have studied biblical truths, and along the way, I have learned many lessons.

In all of my practice, studies and learning on the subject, the one thing that stands out above them all is this: a leader must be ready to make the tough decision. I would add to that, you really are not a leader until you have had to make the tough decision and have made it, come what may.

Former president Ronald Reagan once had an aunt who took him to a cobbler for a pair of new shoes. The cobbler asked young Reagan, "Do you want square toes or round toes?" Unable to decide, Reagan didn't answer, so the cobbler gave him a few days. Several days later the cobbler saw Reagan on the street and asked him again what kind of toes he wanted on his shoes. Reagan still couldn't decide so the shoemaker replied, "Well, come by in a couple of days. Your shoes will be ready."

When the future president did so, he found one square-toed and one round-toed shoe! "This will teach you to never let people make decisions for you," the cobbler said to his indecisive customer. "I learned right then and there," Reagan said later, "if you don't make your own decisions, someone else will."[4]

In the context of our growing social network, leaders are more prone than ever not to make the tough call, to simply let things go. After all, once it is done, the Twitter and Facebook world will all know and weigh in on your decision.

---

[4] Today in the Word, MBI, August 1991, p. 16

Leadership finds itself in this position because we have now confused popularity with leadership.

Please know that popularity and leadership are as far apart as the heavens are above the earth. The two are not joined at the hip. Those of us that are placed in a leadership position by God are not in a popularity contest. Jesus was popular as long as he was providing fishes and loaves; however, when He had to make the tough decisions, popularity subsided and the cry to crucify Him reached a sadistic crescendo.

So, what is a leader to do? Make the call—follow through and make the tough decision! Theodore Hesburgh has a great perspective on this. He says, "My basic principle is that you don't make decisions because they are easy, you don't make them because they are cheap, you don't make them because they're popular, you make them because they're right."

That's right; we make decisions because they are right! All the voices around you may say "Don't do it." Facebook may blow up and Twitter may go crazy, but you must make the call. At the end of the day it isn't the voice of those on Twitter, Facebook or those around you that matter, it's the voice of God saying, "Well done, my good and faithful servant," that matters the most!

During World War II, Winston Churchill was forced to make a painful choice. The British secret service had broken the Nazi code and informed Churchill that the Germans were going to bomb Coventry. He had two alternatives: (1) evacuate the citizens and save hundreds of lives at the expense of indicating to the Germans that the code was broken; or (2) take no action, which would kill hundreds but keep the information flowing and possibly save many more lives. Churchill had to choose and followed the second course.[5]

Today, determine to lead by making the tough call!

------

[5] Between Two Truths - Living with Biblical Tensions, Klyne Snodgrass, 1990, Zondervan Publishing House, p. 179

1. WHAT IS THE _PRINCIPLE_ OF THE LESSON?
My takeaway from the lesson is...

____

____

____

____

____

2. WHAT IS THE _PRACTICE_ FOR ME FROM THE LESSON?
I am committed to doing...

____

____

____

____

3. WHAT IS MY _PRAYER_ AS A RESULT OF THE LESSON?
I am asking God to...

____

____

____

____

DAY 34

Put a Handle on it

I was born in 1958 and grew up in the South. Hattiesburg, Mississippi is the place I call home.

Since my mother traveled a lot, I lived with my grandmother. During the summer, I would go and live with my mother in whatever city and state she was living in at the time. It was a good life; a kind of hybrid life. I was exposed to big city living and Southern hospitality.

During those days, for African Americans in particular, and society as a whole, respect was major. In Nana's house (that's what we called my grandmother), I was taught to respect everyone, even the people with whom I disagreed. This kind of respect was not just a Southern thing. Whenever I would visit my mother in the North, she would demand that I say, *Yes sir, Yes ma'am, Mr., Miss,* and *Mrs.* when addressing adults. Whenever I, or any child for that matter, would forget to do that, the elders would say, "Put a handle on that."

This trip down memory lane was brought to me by US Senator Lindsey Graham of South Carolina and US Congressman Tim Scott of the First District of South Carolina. They were guests on a "Meet the Press" program I was watching, and both are conservative Republicans: one African American and the other white. Both are strongly against President Obama. However, in the context of their comments on the program, there was a big difference in the way they addressed issues concerning the President.

Whenever Senator Graham, the white gentleman, was asked a question, he would always respond by saying "Obama." Whenever Congressman Scott, the African American gentleman, was asked a question, he would respond by saying "President Obama." They both agreed on all the issues and the desire to see President Obama defeated, but only one put a handle on it . . . "President."

Now, this wasn't the first time I had noticed how our President is addressed. I think he will go down in history as not only the first African American President, but also the most disrespected president in our history. Who will forget Representative Joe Wilson interrupting the President's State of the Union Address in 2009 by shouting, "You lie!" And yet, this issue is symptomatic of today's culture. We have lost so much respect for leadership that we no longer even respect the highest office in this land of ours.

We have come to a place in our leadership culture where we are only willing to respect those that agree with our ideas. Clark Clifford shares this reminiscence of his former boss, Harry S. Truman:

Every morning at 8:30 the President would have a staff meeting. One day the mail clerk brought in a lavender envelope with a regal wax seal and flowing purple ribbons. Opening it, the President found a letter from King Ibn Saud of Saudi Arabia, whose salutation began, "Your Magnificence."

"Your Magnificence," Truman repeated, laughing. "I like that. I don't know what you guys call me when I'm not here, but it's okay if you refer to me from now on as 'His Magnificence.'"

Truman subsequently sent a message to the United Nations supporting the admission of 100,000 Jews into Palestine. Soon afterward he received a second letter from King Ibn Saud. This one began: "Dear Mr. President."

One of the core competencies of leadership is respect. Not just the respect you demand for yourself but the respect you deposit into others. Perhaps the biggest reason for the decline in respect that our broader culture has for leadership is due to the leaders' disrespect for other leaders. Leaders have to learn to respect one another. Bono is quoted as saying, "To be one, to be united is a great thing. But to respect the right to be different is maybe even greater."

Thank God for Congressman Tim Scott who reminds us that you can passionately disagree with a leader without being passionately disrespectful. Congressman Scott, thank you for "putting a handle on it." Nana would be proud of you.

1. WHAT IS THE _PRINCIPLE_ OF THE LESSON?

My takeaway from the lesson is...

____

____

____

____

____

2. WHAT IS THE _PRACTICE_ FOR ME FROM THE LESSON?

I am committed to doing…

____

____

____

____

3. WHAT IS MY _PRAYER_ AS A RESULT OF THE LESSON?

I am asking God to…

____

____

____

____

DAY 35

The Dignity of Humanity

Those that know me will tell you of my love for the narrative of history. Two of my favorite quotes on this subject are:

Victor Hugo's words, "What is history? An echo of the past in the future; a reflex from the future on the past."

And Mark Yost's, "History, although sometimes made up of the few acts of the great, is more often shaped by the many acts of the small."

Most of us spend so much time responding to the moment that we never consider how one decision will affect the metanarrative of our history. I believe that when history takes pen to paper and writes of the triumphs of America, at the core of each will be our belief in human dignity. Likewise, when history takes pen to paper and writes of America's shame, at the core of each will be our denial or minimizing of said dignity.

The tapestry that is America is woven together by the common belief in the thread of human dignity. Dr. King knew this and believed this. He once said, "I have decided to stick with love. Hate is too great a burden to bear."

This belief was a part of the construct, orthodoxy and orthopraxy of Dr. Martin Luther King, Jr. and the civil rights movement. Faced with the huge mission of challenging America to live out her creed on behalf of all of her citizens, they armed themselves with belief in human dignity while their enemies armed themselves with instruments of violence that matched their own vicious dispositions.

Armed with the belief in the value of human dignity and the willingness to sacrifice thereunto, Dr. King wrote "Letters From a Birmingham Jail."

Armed with this belief and the willingness to sacrifice thereunto, people of the movement gave their backs to the blistering water from the fire hoses and their faces to the brutal punches of Bull Conner ideologies.

Armed with this belief and the willingness to sacrifice thereunto, Jewish leaders like Abraham Joshua Herschel, Lutheran Pastors like Robert Graetz, Catholic leaders like Bill Hansen and Protestants in general, locked arms and steps with Dr. King and lifted their voices to a sweet crescendo of praise and ushered in a new generation's belief in the words:

We hold these truths to be self-evident, that all men are created equal, that they are endowed by their Creator with certain unalienable rights, that among these are Life, Liberty, and the pursuit of Happiness. I believe those words today because of their efforts yesterday!

Armed with this belief and the willingness to sacrifice thereunto, they sung with hope the songs of Zion; while southern trees were still bearing strange fruit, while blood remained on the leaves and at the root . . . while Black bodies swung in the southern breeze and strange fruit hung from the poplar trees. They still believed in the thread of human dignity . . . even to the point of loving their enemies!

Armed with this belief, Dr. King and this band of citizens and constituents of the movement changed the world!

To deny the reality of this belief in the thread of human dignity, and this aspect of the historicity and legacy of Dr. Martin Luther King Jr. in particular and the civil rights movement in general, makes us at best, revisionist historians and at worst, existential nihilists. And parenthetically, it may be the latter that best describes this current cultural conundrum in which we now live.

Ours is a culture that has in a multitude and a multiplicity of ways lost sight of the very thing that makes us great, our belief in human dignity. Leadership today is more about party politics and less about this human dignity. Great leadership must always begin with a great view of people; and from that lofty paradigm, great leadership always asks of us something great!

About 150 years ago, President Lincoln was returning home from church when an aide asked him how he liked the sermon. Mr. Lincoln responded that he thought the message was well prepared and thoughtfully constructed but that it lacked the most important ingredient. His companion inquired what that might be. Lincoln responded, "The preacher failed to ask us to do anything great."

As a leader, allow your leadership to reflect a high view of people. From that platform, ask of yourself and of those you lead something great. You can do it!

1. WHAT IS THE _PRINCIPLE_ OF THE LESSON?
My takeaway from the lesson is...

____

____

____

____

____

2. WHAT IS THE _PRACTICE_ FOR ME FROM THE LESSON?
I am committed to doing...

____

____

____

____

3. WHAT IS MY _PRAYER_ AS A RESULT OF THE LESSON?

I am asking God to…

____

____

____

____

____

DAY 36

Happiness is Overrated

In the September 14, 1992, issue of *Forbes Magazine*, Peggy Noonan, former speechwriter for Ronald Reagan and correspondent for CBS, wrote:

I think we have lost the old knowledge that happiness in this life is overrated. We have lost the sense of mystery about us, our purpose, or meaning, our role. Our ancestors believed in two worlds, and understood this to be a solitary, poor, nasty, brutish, and short one. We are the first generation of man to actually expect to find happiness here on earth, and our search for it has caused such unhappiness. The reason: If you do not believe in another, higher world, if you believe only in the flat material world around you, if you believe that this is your only chance at happiness, then when the world does not give you a good measure of its riches, you are not disappointed, you are despairing.

I remember reading Peggy's observation for the first time and saying aloud "Amen." The fact is that much of our life today is dictated by our desire to be happy and many lead with happiness as the goal. The construct of happiness envelops our entire life, and instead of asking, "What can we do for our country, community, church and family?" we find ourselves asking what they can do for us.

Leaders that lead to be happy discover that their dividends are limited to situations and circumstances of their leadership sphere. Conversely, those that lead for the joy of the call upon their life experience the compound interest of a joy that is not based upon situations or circumstances. Instead, it is based on the prospect that the world is a better place because they did their part to make it so. Leading to be happy is more often frustrating. Leading for the joy of fulfilling your life mission can be frustrating, but it's simultaneously fascinating, fun, and fulfilling.

Leading for the joy of it requires an emotional intelligence that many just do not get today. We have substituted leading for the joy that is set before us for the happiness we desire now. Someone asked me why I still lived on the south side of town, given all the trouble there. I responded, "I have no choice."

This person interpreted that to mean that I didn't have the money to move and responded, "I am sure I can help you get a loan." "The issue is not money, but mission," I responded. "Are you happy?" they continued. "Happiness is overrated, I am fulfilled," I answered quickly. Needless to say, they didn't understand, so I just asked for the money for a project I was doing and they were "happy" to help.

Today, as a leader, have the courage to lead for the joy that is set before you and not for the happiness that is situational. You'll be following in the footsteps of George Bernard Shaw, who is quoted as saying:

This is the true joy in life, the being used for a purpose recognized by yourself as a mighty one: the being thoroughly worn out before you are thrown on the scrap heap and being a force of nature instead of a feverish selfish little clod of ailments and grievances, complaining that the world will not devote itself to making you happy.[6]

I prefer a mightier purpose, and I hope you do, too.

[6] George Bernard Shaw, quoted in Courage: You Can Stand Strong in the Face of Fear, Jon Johnston, 1990, SP Publications, p. 171.

1. WHAT IS THE _PRINCIPLE_ OF THE LESSON?

My takeaway from the lesson is...

____

____

____

____

____

____

2. WHAT IS THE _PRACTICE_ FOR ME FROM THE LESSON?

I am committed to doing…

____

____

____

____

____

3. WHAT IS MY _PRAYER_ AS A RESULT OF THE LESSON?

I am asking God to…

____

____

____

____

____

DAY 37

Rain Makers

From Tubman to Tupac and beyond, leaders have inspired us to dream.

Harriet Tubman once said, "Every great dream begins with a dreamer. Always remember, you have within you the strength, the patience, and the passion to reach for the stars to change the world. " Tupac Shakur is quoted as saying, "Reality is wrong. Dreams are for real."

As leaders, we spend a lot of time trying to convince ourselves and others that dreams are real. We encourage ourselves and others to pray, work hard and expect dreams to come true. We cheer others on to be who God has created them to be and to follow their heart. However, there are times when we major in inspiration and minor in information and instruction. We inspire people to pray and expect rain, but we do very little in instructing them on how to deal with the mud. Perhaps the amount of rain we prepare others and ourselves to receive is directly related to the amount of mud we prepare both ourselves and them to handle.

Leaders are dealers of hope, so of course we spend a lot of our time planting seeds of hope in those that we see potential in and feel called to influence. However, as dealers of hope, we must be curators of reality. Allow me to put it this way; as I have walked down memory lane, I think the biggest challenge to the success that I have had is the mud slide that followed.

Honestly, I was very naive. I believed that everyone was happy for the things that I was attempting to do and the success I had, especially coming from where I came from. After all, I wasn't ego tripping, I was fulfilling my call. I thought the knife in the back would come from those downtown and across town; but in truth, it came from all around. I was not prepared for the mud of people not liking me, lying about me, setting traps for me, and just down right using me. The more success I experienced, the more momentum the mud slide gained.

I once went into a meeting and was promised by the department head that they were committed to helping with a project. Before I could get out of the city parking lot, a member of her staff phoned my cell and said, "Please don't tell anyone, but she came back into the office after walking you to the elevator and told everyone that we won't be helping you do anything." "Why?" I asked. "Because your idea was better than hers," she replied. This was mud that I was not prepared for. I let it go, because as a child, I was told not to play in the mud. But I must admit, the mud from that situation did get into my eyes.

I was walking in the mall one day. and a young lady stopped me and asked me to try a new product. She went on to say that it was made from the mud of the Dead Sea, and she gave me a history lesson on the healing power of the salt and mud found there. I listened to her presentation and walked away with a thank you.

As I continued walking, I started to think about the lesson she had just taught me about mud. Growing up we were told not to play in the mud—yet now people are paying major dollars for a mud bath. They have learned that there are major beautifying and purifying ingredients in certain kinds of mud.

I smiled to myself at the thought that the mud of my life could be used by God to beautify, purify, and electrify me for bigger and better things. The mud that had gotten into my eyes a few days before was for the purpose of clarifying my vision. Now, I still don't play in the mud, but I am more aware than ever before that every bit of mud that God allows into my life has a medicinal purpose.

So, continue to pray for rain and when the mud comes, know that it is there to beautify, purify and electrify you for bigger and better things. You may pay a price for mud baths, but in the end, they allow you to be you and nobody else.

1. WHAT IS THE *PRINCIPLE* OF THE LESSON?

My takeaway from the lesson is...

____

____

____

____

____

2. WHAT IS THE *PRACTICE* FOR ME FROM THE LESSON?

I am committed to doing…

____

____

____

____

____

3. WHAT IS MY *PRAYER* AS A RESULT OF THE LESSON?

I am asking God to…

____

____

____

____

____

DAY 38

Ubuntu

There is an African concept called *Ubuntu.* The word has its origin in the Bantu languages of southern Africa, and the idea within the word is viewed as a classical African concept.

Archbishop Desmond Tutu offered a definition in a 1999 book:

A person with Ubuntu is open and available to others, affirming of others, does not feel threatened that others are able and good, for he or she has a proper self-assurance that comes from knowing that he or she belongs in a greater whole and is diminished when others are humiliated or diminished, when others are tortured or oppressed.

Tutu further explained Ubuntu in 2008:

One of the sayings in our country is Ubuntu—the essence of being human. Ubuntu speaks particularly about the fact that you can't exist as a human being in isolation. It speaks about our interconnectedness. You can't be human all by yourself, and when you have this quality, Ubuntu, you are known for your generosity. We think of ourselves far too frequently as just individuals, separated from one another, whereas you are connected and what you do affects the whole world. When you do well, it spreads out; it is for the whole of humanity.

In many settings today, we have lost a sense of what we are together or, if you would, *Ubuntu.* I would add to this that I believe there is no other group who so frequently thinks of themselves as *individuals* more than us men. We have been spoon-fed a constant diet of "rugged individualism," and it has cost and continues to cost us dearly.

Rugged individualism is the zeitgeist of our time, and it has as its womb the hearts of men who, in the words of the cybernetically-enhanced humanoid drones of Star Trek the Borg, resist being a part of the "collective." However, "resistance is fertile."

Every great leader, no matter the context of his or her leadership sphere, understands and practices Ubuntu. A leader's heart holds the belief that each one is a part of the collective. The most misunderstood aspect of this, and the force that keeps leaders from working together, is the belief that I have to divorce myself from my individuality to function as a part of the collective. This lie has stifled and stops forward progress, collaborative efforts, and great ideas perhaps more than anything. It is within this context that I believe any given person's leadership depth cannot be determined until he or she has had to lead leaders.

The most challenging aspect of leadership is not getting people to the table—but getting them to work together once they leave the table. To harness the energy of twelve and make it a force of one is about cultivating buy-in. This is achieved by building upon one true, trusted and tested relationship at a time. In *Le Morte d'Arthur: King Arthur and the Legends of the Round Table*, the following is stated:

This is the oath of a Knight of King Arthur's Round Table and should be for all of us to take to heart. I will develop my life for the greater good. I will place character above riches, and concern for others above personal wealth, I will never boast, but cherish humility instead, I will speak the truth at all times, and forever keep my word, I will defend those who cannot defend themselves, I will honor and respect women, and refute sexism in all its guises, I will uphold justice by being fair to all, I will be faithful in love and loyal in friendship, I will abhor scandals and gossip—neither partake nor delight in them, I will be generous to the poor and to those who need help, I will forgive when asked, that my own mistakes will be forgiven, I will live my life with courtesy and honor from this day forward.

Now that's Ubuntu! Some of the greatest achievements of my life have been done alongside of people I thought I never could work with—all because we checked our egos at the door and embraced and cherished humility. We were open and available to each other. We made it our business to affirm one another and not to feel threatened by one another. As a result, not only is there a legacy to what we achieved together, but our victories are much sweeter and more memorable.

I hope the same for you.

1. WHAT IS THE _PRINCIPLE_ OF THE LESSON?

My takeaway from the lesson is...

____

____

____

____

____

2. WHAT IS THE _PRACTICE_ FOR ME FROM THE LESSON?

I am committed to doing…

____

____

____

____

____

3. WHAT IS MY _PRAYER_ AS A RESULT OF THE LESSON?

I am asking God to…

____

____

____

____

____

DAY 39

Dress Code Required

The hotel I was staying at while in Santo Domingo, Dominican Republic had an awesome restaurant. And my place at a table came with my vacation package.

Knowing I had to make reservations a day in advance, I placed one and then arrived there for my 6:30 pm reservation. The young lady at the desk said, "Mr. Payton, we have your reservation, but there is a dress code." She then showed me the small print of my reservation ticket.

I had on a pair of Tommy Bahama pants, Gucci loafers (no socks) and a Gucci short sleeve shirt. So, you may ask, what was the problem? The Tommy Bahama pants were down to the knees shorts. I couldn't be mad, though, because it was in the small print: "No shorts." It wasn't their fault that I didn't read it! They didn't care that I was on vacation. It was simply the rule. It didn't matter how much I paid for them or whose name was on the label. No shorts were allowed!

So, I went back to my room, pulled off the Tommy's and put on a pair of slacks and a Nautica shirt. I kept the Gucci slip-ons (this time with socks). Walking back, I was allowed in with a smile!

Why am I sharing this? Because it reminds me of the sovereignty of God. God invites everyone to the table. But He has one rule: you must be clothed appropriately. That's His sovereign prerogative. Romans 13:14 says, "Rather, clothe yourselves with the Lord Jesus Christ." It doesn't say clothe yourself with Gucci or Tommy Bahama or Prada. It doesn't say clothe yourself in good works. The text says, "Rather, clothe yourselves with the Lord Jesus Christ." This isn't fine print. It's there for all of us to see. It's the rule.

The problem for most of us is that what we're willing to do for entrance into a restaurant or a club, we aren't willing to do for entrance into heaven. We want into God's Kingdom wearing our own attire! Adam and Eve attempted the very same thing. They sewed together fig leaves, and from that moment on, mankind has sought a place at God's table with fig leaf religion.

The main mission of those who lead churches and the mission of every believer is to do as the young lady did to me at the restaurant on vacation. We are to remind all that there is a dress code. We have to tell the king he doesn't have the right clothes on. In the words of Max DePree, "The first responsibility of a leader is to define reality." And Richard J. Mouw writes in *Uncommon Decency*, "Leaders need to have a good picture of what is really going on around them. And they need to help others take an honest look at this reality."

Russian novelist Leo Tolstoy told of an aunt who hurt him deeply when she didn't take time to answer some questions that were troubling him. She stirred his emotions by telling him of Jesus' crucifixion, but when he cried out, "Auntie, why did they torture Him?" she said simply, "They were wicked." "But wasn't He God?" Tolstoy asked. Instead of explaining that Jesus was indeed God, that He had become a man so He could die for our sins, she said, "Be still—it is 9 o'clock!" When he persisted, she retorted, "Be quiet, I say, I'm going to the dining room to have tea." This left young Tolstoy greatly agitated.

Commenting on this scene, Calvin Miller said, "Tolstoy found it incomprehensible that Christ had been brutalized and his aunt was not interested enough to stay a little past teatime and talk about it."

As a leader, as a believer, what are you willing to do? I think it is past time for us to talk about being clothed in the Lord Jesus Christ. How will you invite those in your circle of influence to come clothed in the right attire?

1. WHAT IS THE _PRINCIPLE_ OF THE LESSON?

My takeaway from the lesson is...

____

____

____

____

____

2. WHAT IS THE _PRACTICE_ FOR ME FROM THE LESSON?

I am committed to doing...

____

____

____

____

3. WHAT IS MY _PRAYER_ AS A RESULT OF THE LESSON?

I am asking God to...

____

____

____

____

DAY 40

The Privilege and Responsibility of Your Name

Dear Son,

It has been my honor to know you as my son. From the moment your mother shared the news of her pregnancy with me, I was convinced that God was giving me a son. While you were in your mother's womb, I prayed for you daily and have continued that pattern for nearly 27 years and 9 months now, and I will continue to do so as long as the Lord allows me to tarry here. Just as convinced as I was that God was granting me the responsibility and privilege of a son, I was equally convinced that he would prepare you for great things. I have always expected greater works from you than anything I have done or will ever do. So much so, that perhaps the greatest honor bestowed upon me is being your father.

You should know that I have not known a day where I didn't love you and believe in you. I have tried to raise you according to your particular bent, while also allowing God to define that bent. My goal hasn't been to make up for my mistakes and missed opportunities through you, but to establish an atmosphere for you to define and determine your True North. I have made many mistakes in this. There are meetings I wish I had missed just to spend more time with you. There are times that my desire to provide undercut your desire for my presence. I should have attended more of your basketball games. I should have learned to play video games. There is a multitude and a multiplicity of things I wish I could get a do-over for. But of course, I can't. I would gladly climb the rooftops of the world and cry aloud to you: "I am sorry."

Please understand that my blunders as your father can never blot out the blessing of your Heavenly Father. One of the most prominent signs of this is the mother that He gave you. God gave me an incredible wife and you and your sister an incredible mother. Your respect for women in general should spring forth as a mighty rushing wind because of the mother God has given you.

You must honor and respect that reality because it's the right thing to do and your blessings are attached to it. Ours is a legacy of strong, giving, loving and compassionate black women. In the absence of a father in my life, God provided me with such a mother. In the blunders that I have made as your father, God has provided you, too, with such a mother. Respect her, honor her and thank God for her. Through her, God chose to give you life, and she gave you your name: Zachary, "God remembers," and Ian "gift from God."

My mother didn't have much money to give me, but she gave me a good name, and she along with her two sisters and my grandmother reminded me of it almost daily. I remember sitting on my mother's knee as a child and her telling me the Latin meaning of Anthony, "highly praiseworthy," and the Latin meaning of Payton was "regal." It was later that I learned she thought I was so "highly praiseworthy" that she named me Anthony Tony, which is essentially the same name twice.

As a child, my responsibility to the family name was drilled into me. I was not to do anything that would dishonor the family name. As I grew older and went through my Black Power stage, I questioned my allegiance to the family's slave name. My grandmother would say to me, "Your job is to bring dignity to the name, despite the situation in which it was given to us. You own the name now."

God knows I miss my grandmother.

Zachary, it is past time for you to take ownership of the family name. Your sister's name will change one day. You have been given the stewardship and the responsibility of the family's name. I have tried to pass it to you unblemished. I have tried to conduct myself in a way that you and your children's children would benefit from the favor of our name. You are charged to do the same.

The primary way you accomplish this is by honoring the God whose name is above every name. In His name is the true identity of your name. He has a call upon your life. Fundamentally, it is a call of leadership. You will not be able to escape or divorce yourself from it. The enemy will try to convince you that this call limits your life. He is a liar. The Lord's call does not limit your life, it lifts your life. Will it be difficult? Yes. Will it be challenging? Yes. Will there be times when you feel unappreciated? Yes. However, this call will never limit your life. Please trust me in this. Of the few passing grades that I have in this life, this is chief among them.

Son, you have to lead. The preservation of the family name and the reason that our ancestors survived the Middle Passage and four hundred years of slavery in this country is for such a time as this in your life and the life of your children's children's children. The leadership that you are called to is as a servant leader. Ours is a legacy that will never be based on money, but mission. That's where true riches lie. Make no mistake about it, I want you to experience financial riches, but I don't want you to mistake financial riches with being rich. Love God and His people and you will never be broke. Dismiss God and disregard His people and even with money in the bank, you will still be broke.

We are servant leaders. That's our lot. That's where the Payton name gets its "regal." This is where Zachary will always know "God remembers," and this is the context in which others will know that Ian is "a gift from God." I have written every word of this book with you in mind, and I dedicate it to the greatest leader I have had the privilege to know . . . you. Why do I say this when you have so much life before you? Because I believe it, therefore I speak it, and in your name.

Love You,
Dad.

1. WHAT IS THE *PRINCIPLE* OF THE LESSON?

My takeaway from the lesson is...

____

____

____

____

____

2. WHAT IS THE *PRACTICE* FOR ME FROM THE LESSON?

I am committed to doing…

____

____

____

____

____

3. WHAT IS MY *PRAYER* AS A RESULT OF THE LESSON?

I am asking God to…

____

____

____

____

____